BUTTAL & REBUTTAL
A COLLISION OF BELIEF AND UNBELIEF

Phillip A. Ross

Marietta, Ohio

Copyright ©2016 Phillip A. Ross
All rights reserved.

ISBN: 978-0-9839046-7-0
Edition: 2016-4-10

Published by

Pilgrim Platform
149 E. Spring St., Marietta
Ohio, 45750
www.pilgrim-platform.org

Biblical quotations are from the English Standard Version, Standard Bible Society, unless otherwise cited.

Printed in the United States of America

For my brothers-in-law

J. Mark Taylor
G. Tom Kell

Pilgrim Platform Books

The Work At Zion—A Reckoning, Two-volume set, 772 pages, 1996.
Practically Christian—Applying James Today, 135 pages, 2006.
The Wisdom of Jesus Christ in the Book of Proverbs, 482 pages, 2006.
Marking God's Word—Understanding Jesus, 324 pages, 2006.
Acts of Faith—Kingdom Advancement, 326 pages, 2007.
Informal Christianity—Refining Christ's Church, 136 pages, 2007.
Engagement—Establishing Relationship in Christ, 104 pages, 1996, 2008.
It's About Time! — The Time Is Now, 40 pages. 2008.
The Big Ten—A Study of the Ten Commandments, 105 pages, 2001, 2008.
Arsy Varsy—Reclaiming The Gospel in First Corinthians, 406 pages, 2008.
Varsy Arsy—Proclaiming The Gospel in Second Corinthians, 356 pages, 2009.
Colossians—Christos Singularis, 278 pages, 2010.
Rock Mountain Creed—The Sermon on the Mount, 310 pages, 2011.
The True Mystery of the Mystical Presence, 435 pages, 2011.
Peter's Vision of Christ's Purpose in First Peter, 340 pages, 2011.
Peter's Vision of The End in Second Peter, 184 pages, 2012.
The Religious History of Nineteenth Century Marietta, Thomas Jefferson Summers, 124 pages, 1903, 2012 (editor).
Conflict of Ages—The Great Debate of the Moral Relations of God and Man, Edward Beecher, 489 pages, 1853, 2012 (editor).
Concord Of Ages—The Individual And Organic Harmony Of God And Man, Edward Beecher, D. D., 524 pages, 1860, 2013 (editor).
Ephesians—Recovering the Vision of a Sustainable Church in Christ, 417 pages, 2013.
Poet Tree—Root, Branch & Sap, 72 pages, 2013.
Inside Out Woman—Collected Poetry, Doris M. Ross, 195 pages, 2014 (editor).
Buttal And Rebuttal—A Collision of Belief and Unbelief, 140 pgs. 2015
Galatians—Backstory/Christory, 230 pgs, 2015

Table of Contents

Introduction..1
Buttal & Rebuttal..7
Postscript...130
Appendix..139

INTRODUCTION

Several years ago I found myself in a conversation that provided an opportunity to defend the faith (1 Peter 3:15). The presenting concern was about homosexuality, but it quickly moved to the underlying Godless worldview that motivates various kinds of perversion. The other person is not personally known to me, nor is his personal identity important to the argument—nor is mine. He simply represents the voice of an educated atheist, though he called himself a skeptic.

I have reproduced that discussion here as a study of competing worldviews because it provided me with an opportunity to speak about my understanding of Christianity in a way that I haven't done before. And it provides an in-depth exposure of the ideas inherent in the growing movement of Modern Atheism.[1] In this regard, it exposes some of the misunderstandings of Christianity that are fueling this movement, and might provide some guidance about how to address some of these issues in a more productive way. However, I was unable to sway my opponent as far as I know. Nor did he sway me.

The discussion has been edited slightly in order to make it flow better by removing extraneous elements and correcting spelling and punctuation, which are often casualties of modern social communication technologies. For the most part, it has been reproduced just as it happened over a couple of months. I pray that it will be helpful to those who find it.

---

1   Buckley. Michael J. *At the Origins of Modern Atheism*, Yale University Press, 1990. Also: http://en.wikipedia.org/wiki/New_Atheism.

Science is not as cut and dried as many non-scientists suppose. To show this I include this quote from Bill Bryson's popular 2004 book, *A Short History of Nearly Everything*:

> "The upshot of all of this is that we live in a universe whose age we can't quite compute, surrounded by stars whose distances we don't altogether know, filled with matter we can't identity, operating in conformance with physical laws whose properties we don't truly understand" (p. 172).

Because I argue presuppositionally in the following pages, and because presuppositionalism is not well-understood, I have also included a blog post that might help people better understand my methodology.

A Presuppositionalist Parable: You'll Be Floored[2]

I've been listening most recently to some of Sye ten Bruggencate's apologetic debates and conversations. My goal is always to become a more effective apologist, myself. I'll confess that I spend a lot of time admiring him and his partners and thinking how poorly I'd have done in that situation. But I keep at it, because it's both a Christian's calling and part of the task of being a pastor, whether it comes easily to one or not.

Presuppositionalist apologists like Sye and others argue insistently (and to their opponents' dismay) that anti-Christians' every argument denying God's existence, in fact, proves God's existence. The point is a very good one, but I'm not sure everyone gets it.

Me, I'm simple; so I always chew things over to the point of my own understanding ... and by that time, I've got something just about anyone can understand. Usually a good analogy helps me. Here, I think I have one, so I offer it to you, with the disclaimer that every analogy breaks down at some point.

---

[2] http://teampyro.blogspot.com/2013/05/a-presuppositionalist-parable-youll-be.html. Dan Phillips pastors Copperfield Bible Church in Houston, TX, is author of *The World-Tilting Gospel* (Kregel, 2011) and *God's Wisdom in Proverbs* (Kress, 2011), and writes at the blog Pyromaniacs, from which the parable above is taken.

For starters, presups point out that God is not a conclusion, He's the starting-place. Unbelievers hear this as saying we've no proof of God, though it isn't what we're saying nor meaning. I've wondered whether it might not be more effective to say that the truth of God is too big and fundamental to be the conclusion of a syllogism or chain of reasoning. Only truths of a certain size can fit at the end of a chain of reasoning, and the truth of God is too big to come at the end. That truth is so big and fundamental that it only fits at the start; any other location whittles that truth down to unrecognizability.

So here's the analogy. Envision two philosophical combatants. One school, the Floorists, asserts the existence of the floor as that on which everything else necessarily rests. The other (Afloorists) denies that assertion.

The Floorists say, "If there were no floor, we wouldn't even be here. We'd be nowhere. There'd be no connecting-point and no common-ground—literally. And you Afloorists confirm that fact with every word."

The Afloorists scoff. "Prove there's a floor, without standing on one!"

Floorists: "Can't do that."

Afloorists: "Aha! You see? You have no proof!"

Floorists: "No, we can't do that because we can't even have this discussion without resting on a floor. We can't even talk to you without all of us resting on the floor. The only reason we're talking right now is that both of us are resting on a common floor."

Afloorists: "Nonsense! For instance, look here, I'll show you..." (stepping off the couch onto the floor).

Floorist: "Stop. You just proved the floor. Even before you moved, you proved the floor. You were sitting on something resting on the floor."

Afloorist: "What? I never did! I'm just showing you, here and..." (taking a second step).

Floorist: "Stop! If there's no floor, you couldn't take a first step, let alone a second. All the time your mouth is running, denying the floor, you're standing on the very floor you deny. Every step you take, denying the floor, depends on the floor. You know that, or you'd not have stepped off so confident that something would support you. Every step you take affirms the floor. If there were no floor, you couldn't walk around denying the floor. Every step proves what your mouth denies."

Afloorist: "Bosh. You just can't prove the floor without assuming the floor. You have no evidence. Here, let me show you another place where there's no floor."

Floorist: "Only if you can do it without resting or walking on the floor."

Afloorist: "We can do that! We all know we can do that! Science has proved we can do that! Your problem is that you can't prove there is a floor!"

Floorist: "You can't even say that without resting on the floor. You're denying the floor that you know exists, and meanwhile you're depending on the floor, to deny the floor."

Afloorist (triumphantly): "Aha! You see? You have no proof! You refuse to prove the floor! We ask for evidence, you give none! You don't prove it here (takes step), or here (takes step), or here (jumps up and down). There is no floor! There. Now I'm going to go have sex, thanks to this exhilarating freedom that Afloorism has brought me."

Floorist: "…on something resting on the floor. Brilliant."
[Facepalm.]

There y'go.

Nicely said. The idea is that whatever argument one is pursuing, it rests on various assumptions. And those assumptions are understood in such a way that gives the argument its "rational" foundation.

This discussion has fueled another book that delves deeper into the biblical content in order to address the growing, faulty understanding of the Bible that drives the New Atheists and much faulty Christianity. Think of it as a companion volume that addresses the much misunderstood issue of law and gospel presented by Paul to the Galatians. I call it *Galatians—Backstory/Christory*, Pilgrim Platform, 2016.

Special thanks to Dick Brewer, Bob Springer, and my wife, Stephanie, for proofreading and providing feedback.

Phillip Ross
Marietta, Ohio
January 2016

BUTTAL & REBUTTAL

SIMON: JERRY, IT IS GOOD TO SEE YOU ALL PUSHING CALVINISM AS hard as you can. The rest have compromised saying it does not get the young in church. Or it is to offensive! Keep pushing for Calvinism, Calvin did it and we had a reformation. "Lord willing Calvinism will rule again." Maybe this time it will rule China, and China can convert Islam?

John: Have you guys read the books of Brother Yun? That's his same desire!

Mike: I vote for Jesus ruling!

James: He rules now!

Steven: Jerry, you continually lump homosexuality together with pedophilia and bestiality. You are just wrong about this. As I have pointed out before, homosexual sex between consenting adults, in and of itself, harms no one.[1] Pedophilia is a sexual violation of a minor who cannot reasonably consent to such actions.

---

1 The issue of social harm will increasingly come into play regarding this issue. Traditional emphasis have been on individual harm, i.e., https://en.wikipedia.org/wiki/Harm_principle. Yet social harm has been an area of study for a long time, i.e., https://en.wikipedia.org/wiki/Zemiology. Whether homosexuality contributes to other areas of harm that impact social relationship and contracts, health, medicine, etc. is yet to be determined, i.e., http://whose-law.blogspot.com/2010/10/drug-policy-harm-part-one-social-harm.html.

Likewise, animals cannot consent to acts of bestiality. I would ask you why you continue to make this invalid comparison, but I think the answer is obvious. People are beginning to see past the hate and realize that homosexuality is, in and of itself, a threat to no one. So you are trying to revive the old revulsion by linking them with the lowest of law breakers. You will lose this argument, and the world will be better for it.

Luis: Steven, the problem is not harm against other humans but the sin is against God.

And how can you say pedophilia is bad? Who says it is wrong? There are consenting children also and it has been recorded in scientific journals that they have benefited from pedophilia. Is it society that is supposed to define morality? If it is society, then society can make pedophilia acceptable. Such a thing is comparable to Hitler killing Jews because the German society agreed that killing the Jews was okay.

So as a result the idea that society determines morality is that God does not. And when God is not involved in morality people are free to say anything. We have no protection against pedophilia because pedophiles harm no one.

The plain truth is that America was not founded on the basis of a relativistic mindset, but by individuals influenced by Christianity who knew that morality is objective and social change must be done cautiously. Read *A Queer Thing Happened to America: And What a Long, Strange Trip It's Been*, by Michael L. Brown, Equal Time Books, 2011.

Phillip: You might also read my article on the Definition of Marriage[2] because the definition of terms always determines the shape and conclusion of an argument, case, statement, or policy, assuming that it unfolds logically.

---

2   See Appendix.

Steven: Man, I can't wait until you guys lose this debate so you can move on to something else. Law by semantic definition —that's not what we need!

James: "Know ye not that the unrighteous shall not inherit the kingdom of God? Be not deceived: neither fornicators, nor idolaters, nor adulterers, nor effeminate, nor abusers of themselves with mankind, Nor thieves, nor covetous, nor drunkards, nor revilers, nor extortioners, shall inherit the kingdom of God" (1 Corinthians 6:9-10).

Find out where a nation gets its laws and you will find out what their god is. All law is religion. The question is where you get the authority for law. From the ever-changing heart and mind of depraved men? Or from the giver of life and law itself?

Steven: James, not everyone believes in the divine origins of the Bible. In our great nation, which was founded on Lockean principles of freedom, not on religion or its dogma. Americans do not have to follow the Bible's teachings as a matter of law. In essence, the Bible passages you and others quote have no relevance to the legal question of homosexual rights.

You get your principles from your own mind, just as I get mine from my mind. It is you who has decided to believe that the Bible speaks God's perfect word. Do not try to claim that the positions you are putting forward are objective. They come from beliefs you have chosen to hold for reasons that are no more objective than mine.

Yes all law is religion, but only if you completely redefine the words law and religion.

James: Steven, if we all live in a world with no final authority but our own minds, then right and wrong are determined by how we feel and what the current trends are in society. It is because of this error that we have legalized adultery, sodomy, pornography, and murder (the current illegal wars and abortion) while other good things as described in God's law are made illegal. In short, American society is full of idolaters who frame mischief by law.

Steven: James, you live in exactly the same world I do. Your moral authority is also based on your own brain. It is your brain that has determined to regard the Bible as God's word. Thus it is your brain that proposes these rules. Your system is no different than anyone else's.

James: The reason you do not believe as I do, Steven, is not a matter of your simply choosing to believe. Apparently, God has chosen to leave you in darkness and ignorance. I pray that this changes. The reason I believe is not because I made a choice to do so, but because God in his mercy chose to reveal Christ to me, He brought the light of the gospel which has enabled me to believe. Short of that, the only thing that will settle this issue for us both is death and judgment.

Steven: Do you think that God created billions of people with the deliberate intent of forcing most of them into eternal torment? How do you reconcile this action with the idea that God is love?

Phillip: Steven, actually the legal views and values of the Bible are as close to objectivity that human beings can get. Why? Because the Bible has been the foundation for the most universally accepted principles of law since Moses came down from the mountain. The biblical principles of law—the Ten Commandments, essentially—have been accepted in more nations and cultures over the longest period time than any other. So, they have the most universal approval of humanity in history.
Except during the past fifty or sixty years, when there has been a creative, intelligent, and well-funded public relations campaign to reverse this norm by people who encourage homosexu-

ality. The word queer isn't just about sex, but it means "beyond or deviating from the usual or expected norm."

Of course, my values are in my mind and yours are in your mind. Of course, our opinions are shaped by what we read and hear. But no man is an island. So, if you could read everything ever written through all human history, you would see that homosexuals comprise a very small minority of the world's people at any given time. Why has homosexuality been illegal, overtly or tacitly, in almost every society over almost all of human history? Do you think that all those people were as ignorant, stupid, and gullible as you think Christians are?

And, yes, it is true that homosexuality also has a very long history that dates well before the destruction of Sodom and Gomorrah. But that history is also rife with "sexual immorality, impurity, sensuality, idolatry, sorcery, enmity, strife, jealousy, fits of anger, rivalries, dissensions, divisions, envy, drunkenness, orgies, and things like these" (Galatians 5:19-21). Such things don't make for good social cohesion.

Belief does not make the Bible true, nor does disbelief make it untrue. True things are consistent with reality over time. And because the Bible has been accepted as being true by so many people over so long a time in so many different ages and cultures, the burden of proof is not on Christians to prove that it is true—that's been done quite a bit and the literature is readily available. Rather, the burden of proof is upon unbelievers to prove that it isn't.

Steven: Phillip, you said "The biblical principles of law—the Ten Commandments, essentially—have been accepted in more nations and cultures over the longest period time than any other."

Let's take a closer look at that claim and see how many of the Ten Commandments have influenced laws:

1. "I am the LORD your God, who brought you out of Egypt, out of the land of slavery. You shall have no other gods before me."

Used in our laws? No.

2. "You shall not misuse the name of the LORD your God, for the LORD will not hold anyone guiltless who misuses his name."
Used in our laws? No.

3. "Remember the Sabbath day by keeping it holy."
Used in our laws? No.

4. "Honor your father and your mother."
Used in our laws? No.

5. "You shall not murder."
Used in our laws? Yes.

6. ""You shall not commit adultery."
Used in our laws? No.

7. "You shall not steal."
Used in our laws? Yes.

8. "You shall not give false testimony against your neighbor."
Used in our laws? No.

9. "You shall not covet your neighbor's house."
Used in our laws? No.

10. "You shall not covet your neighbor's wife."
Used in our laws? No.

So, this list of commandments that is supposed to form the foundation of our legal system provides only two laws we use today. Eighty percent of the Ten Commandments are not used in our legal system. Not very foundational, if you ask me.

James: Initially, all of the commandments were the basis of law in the colonies. Idolatry, blasphemy, sabbath breaking, adultery and bearing false witness were all punished to one degree or another. Bearing false witness can get you jail time this very day.

Steven: James, you said "Initially, all of the commandments were the basis of law in the colonies."

Maybe so, but that is a far cry from the claim made by Phillip (and others I've met) who say that the Ten Commandments form the foundation of modern law.

So, to be clear, you are saying that in the Thirteen Colonies there were laws against saying "Jehovah," not being a Christian, not honoring one's parents, working on Saturday, coveting another's goods or wife, and telling lies?

Phillip: Steven, all of your comparisons are about our current United States law, and are the result of the fifty or sixty year period of change I mentioned. Current U.S. law provides a very small sampling of history and of the world's population. But thanks for making my point.

Steven: Oh, I see! Can you provide me with just a couple of examples of the many, many civilizations, other than the ancient Hebrews, who implemented laws against saying "Jehovah," not being a Christian, not honoring one's parents, working on Saturday, coveting another's goods or wife, and telling lies?

Phillip: If you are really interested you would realize that it is a larger project than this discussion forum. Nonetheless, how about Europe, Briton (the historic Empire), South America, Russia. Again, you will have to look beyond the current era.

Steven: There was a law against coveting in those countries? Reference please?

Phillip: Here are a couple of websites that provide this information:
www.faithfacts.org/christ-and-the-culture/the-bible-and-government
www.lonang.com/biblicalprinciples.htm
www.faithfacts.org

Steven: Phillip, this is so silly. Your links go to pages where someone has done their best to match legal principles with their representation in human government and then they've quote-mined the Bible to show that this is really where these things come from. My favorite one is that the system of checks and balances is founded on the principle that all men sin against God. LOL!

Phillip: Steven, your accusation of silliness is a form of scoffing (2 Peter 3:3). What don't you understand about governmental checks and balances being related to sin?

Steven: Yes, I am scoffing at the idea that our Founding Fathers, who built a nation unlike any other in the world because of their devotion to the principles of Lockean liberty, designed our system of checks and balances because the Bible says human beings disobey God. It is a proposition I find quite scoffworthy.

Phillip: John Locke said, "The Bible is one of the greatest blessings bestowed by God on the children of men. It has God for its author; salvation for its end, and truth without any mixture for its matter. It is all pure."

Steven: Locke was a religious man, yes, but he held ideas about government that are very different from yours and that do not assert that God is the authority for government. Read his "Social Contract."

Phillip: What do you know about Covenant Theology? Locke's social contract is a pale, Godless imitation of it.

Steven: I know a little about Covenant Theology and it is almost completely different from Locke's Social Contract. The only thing they have in common is the idea that a contract exists.

That's it. As you say, the Lockean contract on which the U.S. government is based has nothing to do with God.

Phillip: Steven, a covenant is not a contract, though there are similarities. Who did God make His covenant with? The Bible teaches that he made it with humanity, so God's covenant precedes Locke's idea of social contract. It has precedence in both history and extent.

In addition, the Declaration of Independence and the U.S. Constitution are not completely Godless, but are compromise documents between Christians and non-Christians. Neither the Constitution nor the Declaration of Independence explicitly refer to Jesus Christ. However, biblical language and assumptions are rife throughout—except for those who are so unfamiliar with the Bible as to not recognize them. The Founders very intentionally wanted to bring together Christians and non-Christians because they knew that the new nation would not work without both parties. So they alluded to the Bible and God, used the assumptions and teachings of the Bible, but did not use the name of Jesus Christ, and God is only mentioned in the Declaration. Those who don't know what the Bible teaches and assumes can't know this, but their ignorance doesn't effect the reality.

To suggest, as you do, that the U.S. Constitution has nothing to do with God is evidence of historical ignorance and threatens to break the compromise between Christians and non-Christians, just as writing Jesus Christ into the Constitution would break the compromise on the other side. The "non-Christians" in the 1700-1800s were Christian Deists who were okay with the Bible and God, but knew that references to Jesus Christ would set off Christian denominational rivalries, or would encourage Christian unity, which would increasingly mitigate against the non-Christian block. But however you cut it, most of the people of the time were overwhelmingly Christian, though not all were.

Today the U.S. is on the brink of the reversal of this fact and, unlike the more accommodating Christians of yesteryear, the non-Christians of today are quite narrowmindedly working to write every vestige of religious language or allusion out of every federal document and institution. Doing so threatens the compromise of the Constitution itself.

Christians do not want to impose Christianity on non-Christians because doing so goes against Jesus' teachings. Yes, we think it is important to teach the stories and values of the Bible to everyone because of the role of the Bible in the world and American history is important. We are happy to teach this along side of Locke and Hume and the like because we trust that truth itself, freely expressed and discussed, must and will eventually win people to Jesus Christ.

But non-Christians are intent on imposing secularism (the doctrine that rejects religion and religious considerations) upon everyone. That spirit violates the compromise of the U.S. Constitution and tends to undermine the Christian heritage of the nation and of young people, who by the way, are not taught the real history and heritage of the U.S. And that is the real problem.

Steven: Phillip, you said "But non-Christians are intent on imposing secularism (the doctrine that rejects religion and religious considerations) upon everyone."

Please point out these people who want to impose secularism. As far as I can tell, the people who do not want religious references in government are fine with you believing whatever nonsecular things you want. They are fine with you teaching them to others and to your children. What they are not fine with is having our government show a preference for one point of view over another. Keeping silent on the matter is not showing a preference for secularism.

Phillip: But Steven, notice that in the contemporary situation we have gone from the Constitution not using explicit references to Jesus Christ, to the complete eradication of all Christian reference in every aspect of government. That constitutes a huge change, especially when we consider how much that government has encroached into every aspect of life.

Christianity teaches that God impacts every area of life. That is the Christian perspective. The secular perspective teaches that God has no impact whatsoever on any area of life. The Constitution alludes to both perspectives by using biblical teaching, assumptions and allusions, but not making explicit reference to the Bible. That's the compromise. I'm saying that both perspectives need to have the freedom to be freely expressed. And they were for a century or so. You remember the First Amendment and religious freedom, right? Did you know that it was the Christian clergy who insisted on that amendment? It's purpose was not to keep religion out of government, but to keep the government out of religion.

Consider public education: Nearly all education in the U.S. was home schooling at the very beginning—and Christian! Then as churches were established, the churches provided education and included their particular perspectives in their teaching. Over time the government took over public education from the churches by making it "free" (through taxation) and banned all Christian teaching in public schools—in the name of freedom, while diminishing the freedom of Christians to teach their perspective.

You will undoubtedly counter this by saying that public funds are used for public education and the government cannot show religious favoritism, which is true. But let's try this experiment: eliminate all governmental funding for public education and allow each community to fund its own schools at the local level. The Catholics could fund their own. Oh yes, they already do. The Baptists, Methodists, Buddhists, Muslims, etc., could each fund their own, or decide to cooperate. And the atheists could fund their own, of course. Or they could come to a Christian school if there weren't enough atheists to fund a school. That would be okay with Christians. Do you think education would change? I do. And wouldn't it be more fair for each community to have real control than for the federal government force its godless standards on everyone?

As it is, we have a small minority of atheists dictating godless curriculum for the monopoly of government education to the most religious nation on earth. Something is very wrong with a "democracy" like this. The problem is that secular government has taken over most of what has been traditionally done by churches and/or church families—education, health and hospitals (also known as healing), elder care, retirement.

Actually, there are several spheres of cooperative government that should operate in harmony: self-government, also known as conscience, family government, church government, and civil government. But nowadays all government is civil (secular) government. Such a condition is also called secular totalitarianism. And in everything that this secular civil government does, it erases and forbids all mention of God, and especially Jesus Christ —all in the name of freedom, which is supposed to include religious freedom.

You are one of the people who wants to continue to impose secularism. Right?

Steven: Phillip, what you present is not an argument so much as it is a fantasy. This balance that was supposedly struck between a Christian constitution and a secular one never happened. The Constitution is, was and always shall be godless and thank goodness for that. The only "balance" that must be struck is in your own mind. You make ridiculous claims like secular government equals totalitarianism. Phillip, I don't think there's any other way to say it. You have no idea what you're talking about. Making up theories about how the Constitution was written and redefining words to suit you doesn't help your cause.

Mention God all you want. Start a church. Teach your faith to anyone who will listen. You are totally free to do that, but you can't use the government and my tax dollars to do it. If that is not free enough for you, you are in the wrong country.

Phillip: Granted, I'm speaking about things that you are not aware of.

Steven: Then please make me aware. Do you have some evidence to present for your balanced Constitutional theory? Perhaps the authors spoke of this in some notes I have not read. I am very serious here, by the way. I am always willing to reevaluate my stance if I am provided with compelling evidence.

Phillip: Of course, there was no official "deal" struck between the religious and secular forces at the time of the Constitution, as you know. It was more of a tacit, unwritten agreement, like many that occur in the back rooms of political involvement. It goes on today and it went on then. The two sides of the tacit compromise of the time were the conservatives and the liberals, or we could call them the Christians and the Deists. The Constitution was written on the heels of the Great Awakening, so Christianity was very much on people's minds.

Nonetheless, the impetus for the Establishment Clause was to keep the government out of religion rather than to keep religion out of government, evidenced by the fact that the clergy were responsible for it. And today it is the government that is involved in the church rather than the church being involved in the government.

May I suggest that you have two specific misconceptions:

Presentism—The tendency to apply Twenty-First century values and understandings to historical events. You want to believe the Constitution is a secular document because God is not specifically mentioned. But even a cursory search of the writings of any of those present in Philadelphia in 1787 would show they held a profoundly Christian view of society. But because you have a strong socially afflicted aversion to Christianity, you have no idea what this means or the extent of its application. Even the bad Christians (like Alexander Hamilton at this point in his life) had a somewhat biblical view of the world because that was the dominant social view of the age.

God is not mentioned in the document because He is assumed by those involved, as He was in the collective mind of colonial America. People seldom articulate their assumptions. Fish don't realize they are underwater and birds don't consciously reference the wind in order to fly—it's automatic, unconscious, and for this case, it is/was unwritten.

The very fact that the framers accepted some rights as being "natural" specifically implied the existence of God as the giver of those rights because that was the common language of the day that referred to God, at least for Christians who dominated society at the time. An overt atheist in that day would not have gotten anywhere politically.

Solipsism—The tendency to accept nothing as true outside the self. This leads to a misconception of reality and often to the creation of an alternate, more preferable but imaginary reality. Again, you are reading your own values and perspective into the past.

Steven: Phillip, you said "Of course, there was no official 'deal' struck between the religious and secular forces at the time of the Constitution, as you know. It was more of a tacit, unwritten agreement, like many that occur in the back rooms of political involvement."

So, one of those agreements for which there is no evidence whatsoever, like the agreement to fake the moon landing or 911. There is no reason to think this compromise occurred other than that it is assumed to have happened (your word, not mine).

I hope you will not be overly surprised to hear that this approach does not sway me, nor thankfully does it sway Constitutional scholars who seem to prefer more conventional hermeneutics.

If belief in God as the foundation of government was as pervasive as you say, then the argument can reasonably be made that leaving God out of the Constitution was a conscious, deliberate choice. I know that you don't like where the establishment clause has gotten us, but it is where we are and I don't find any compelling evidence that it was not what the framers intended.

Phillip: Steven, I'm simply acknowledging the political reality of the time. You say that you would like to understand my position, but it appears that you have no intention or interest in understanding it.

You are like a Jedi master who attempts to dismiss the obvious with a wave of your hand, and what magicians call redirection. To understand the reality of the Great Awakening and its impact on America, you might have to read a bit.

It is not that there is no evidence for the compromise I mentioned, but the evidence is not like an electrical diagram or building blueprints. Reality is more complicated than that.

I'm not saying that "belief in God" is the foundation of government, I'm saying that the Bible provided the foundation of the American system of government. The roots and history are plain for everyone who is willing to take the time to study it out, whether they believe in God or not.

And, yes, the decision to leave out explicit reference to Jesus Christ was a conscious decision on the part of the Framers. But it was not done in order to remove all vestiges of religious thought or consideration from government. It was in order to keep the government from establishing a church, because of the English Civil War. They did not want a government like that of England, where the king is the head of the church. So, they left reference to Jesus Christ and God out in order to insure that the state would not stake claim to Him.

But actually the U.S. government has established a church or religion known as the American Civil Religion.

So, what about your *presentism* and solipsism?

Steven: *Presentism*—a great, great number of people in the present, yourself included, do not feel that there should be a wall of separation between Church and state, so I don't see how you can claim that I am applying the present standards to our framers. I'm sure it was the same 250 years ago. Even if the prevailing public view was Christian, our founding fathers are noteworthy for having created something new; a government intentionally separate from the institutions of religion and based on social contract theory.

Solipsism—I recognize a great many things outside of myself as true, so I'm not sure I completely understand how you mean this.

This graphic is not totally relevant to our current debate, but I thought it was an interesting commentary on the claim I've often heard in these debates that there can be no moral authority without God.

Society is falling apart because it has lost its God-given sense of right and wrong.

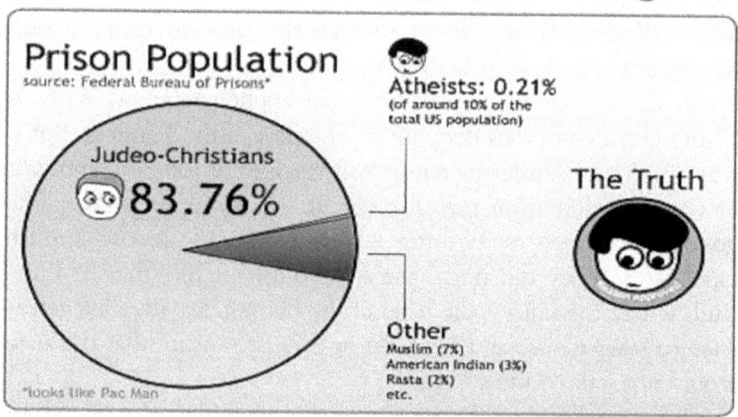

Phillip: You've got me wrong, Steven. I am a staunch supporter of the separation of church and state. I just wish it were a reality. You haven't heard a thing I've been saying. But to cite a cartoon to suggest that the Christianity in prisons is normative Christianity is absurd. In addition, people don't go to jail because they are Christians (most anyway). Rather, they find that they need Christ after screwing up their lives. I would argue that there is no moral authority apart from Jesus Christ, but you'd just blow it off without the slightest concern or effort to actually understand what I mean. So, I won't.

Steven: "You've got me wrong, Stephen. I am a staunch supporter of the separation of church and state. I just wish it were a reality. You haven't heard a thing I've been saying."

Apparently I have not. I thought I read somewhere above that you thought that the Constitution, the foundation of our government, was actually based on the Bible. I also thought you were in favor of a law against homosexual marriage because of your religious beliefs. I must get my ears (eyes?) checked.

Phillip: That's correct, the American system of government is based upon the Bible. But what you don't know is anything about the Bible. The Bible itself is the source of the separation of church and state. The New Testament is different than the Old Testament. Things changed. And regarding homosexual marriage: marriage is not in the jurisdiction of the civil government. Civil government has encroached into the jurisdiction of the family and the church. Civil government should have the authority to register marriages, not to issue licenses. It is not your eyes or ears that need to be checked, but your ignorance and the values that have grown from it.

You might be interested in this article on *The Contested History of American Freedom*.[3]

---

3 http://digitalhistory.hsp.org/pafrm/essay/contested-history-american-freedom.

Steven: "The New Testament is different than the Old Testament. Things changed." But doesn't Jesus tell us that we must still obey the Old Testament law?

Phillip: Steven, that is the question of the century, and I see that you really don't know the answer (though you may think you do). I know that you want a simple, comic book answer, but reality is not so simple. Jesus said:
"For truly, I say to you, until heaven and earth pass away, not an iota, not a dot, will pass from the Law until all is accomplished" (Matthew 5:18).
"But it is easier for heaven and earth to pass away than for one dot of the Law to become void" (Luke 16:17).
"You therefore must be perfect, as your heavenly Father is perfect" (Matt. 5:48)
The answer to your question is in the story of Jesus Christ, and apart from understanding the story, no answer is available. Why? Because the answer has a context, and apart from that context the answer won't be true. And it's a long story that isn't over yet.
Nonetheless, let me throw caution to the wind and pray that I'm not putting pearls before swine as I make it as simple as I can.
God created everything perfect. Satan tricked Eve and then Adam abdicated his responsibility as they believed themselves (their own thoughts and feelings—as you do, Steven), against God's advice. That caused them to fall from the state of innocent righteousness. And because God is perfect and perfection cannot countenance imperfection they were cast out of the Garden. They couldn't "hang" with God anymore because they didn't trust him—because they trusted themselves. Adam and Eve represent humanity in the story because all humanity has come from their loins.
At this point, all humanity born of Adam and Eve are destined for hell because all are sinners. Adam and Eve taught all of their children to do as they had done, and those children taught

their children, etc. So in the Old Testament you see a lot of really bad stuff that God cannot countenance. But this is what God had to work with.

Nonetheless, God loved them in spite of their sin, and has a plan to redeem them—restore their/our perfection. First, understand that "perfection" does not mean what you think it means. It is not a philosophical concept. It is moral.

So, knowing that humanity could not keep His law (the Ten Commandments) perfectly, and knowing that their redemption would require them to keep it perfectly, He gave the law to Moses who gave it to Israel with the demand to "just do it." They tried, and made a wreck of it, which was no surprise to God. He knew that they/we could not keep the Ten Commandments, yet He demands perfect compliance. In other words, God put humanity in an impossible dilemma.

All the Ten Commandments did was to show humanity/individuals the perfection of God's law and the impossibility of their compliance. In other words, the perfection of the law revealed the extent of the sin. Perfect obedience to the law would fix the problem of sin, but no one could do it.

This the context I was talking about. We cannot continue the story unless and until you understand the context. And if we try, as many do, without understanding (and agreeing with) the context, the rest of the story cannot make the sense that God wants it to make of it.

So, are you with me so far?

Steven: Phillip, I don't understand why you are telling me the story of original sin as though you think I might not have not already heard it. Be that as it may, I understand the concept of original sin and am perfectly capable of using it as a context for your statements. I believe your last statement was:

"The New Testament is different than the Old Testament. Things changed."

You also acknowledged, correctly, that Jesus himself demands that the Old Testament law (which you should know full well consists of way more than just the Ten Commandments) must stay in effect and not be changed at all. Christians today should still be stoning people for gathering sticks on Saturday or cursing their parents. I don't think New Covenant theology gets you out of this one but, as always, I eagerly await your next mental gymnastic.

Phillip: Steven, It's not that I don't think that you have heard about original sin, but that I'm not sure you believe it. I'm not suggesting that you have to believe everything in the Bible just as I do. No. However, belief in the sinfulness of humanity and the perfection of God are necessary in order to correctly understand the role of Jesus Christ.

Will you be in church today?

The question is not unwarranted because the Old Testament teaches that worship is to take place on Saturday according to the Fourth Commandment. But Christians worship on Sunday. Something changed.

According to the Old Testament, God's people must not eat a variety of foods, some are clean and some are unclean. However, Peter was instructed to eat all foods (Acts 10). Something changed.

As you say, Old Testament law is comprised of much more than the Ten Commandments. The actual number is more like 613. But Jesus reduced it to two (Luke 10). Something changed.

And yet Jesus also said, "For truly, I say to you, until heaven and earth pass away, not an iota, not a dot, will pass from the Law until all is accomplished. Therefore whoever relaxes one of the least of these commandments and teaches others to do the same will be called least in the kingdom of heaven, but whoever does them and teaches them will be called great in the kingdom of heaven. For I tell you, unless your righteousness exceeds that of the scribes and Pharisees, you will never enter the kingdom of heaven" (Matthew 5:18-20). Both of these statements are true.

I suspect that you have no idea what New Covenant theology is actually about. Indeed, a little mental gymnastics are good for the head muscle—gets the blood flowing. Again, the Old Testament puts humanity into a double bind because we are required to do something that we cannot do. That is the overwhelming conclusion of the Old Testament. But the story is not over yet.

Are you with me so far?

Steven: Wow, not even close to being with you on this. So, Jesus says that we must be even more obedient to the 600 or so laws than the Pharisees, and also instructs Peter to break them. He says we must not change the old law a jot or tittle, then he "reduces them to two." Limber up please, because this kind of glaring, plain-as-the-nose-on-your-face contradiction is going to need some major rationalizing.

And, please, feel free to test me on New Covenant theology. Not agreeing with you does not mean I am not capable of understanding it.

Phillip: Steven, We have not come to how Jesus solves the dilemma yet. And because you don't understand the context, you mangle the New Testament. Jesus said that we must be more obedient than the Pharisees, and their 613 laws, and the way to do that is to concentrate on two: love God and neighbor. But apart from faith in Jesus Christ even that is not possible.

The purpose of the Old Testament was to prepare the world for Jesus Christ. Imagine that it is night and you are preparing for the morning. In the night you light lamps and clean and organize your gear. In the morning when the sun (Son) comes, you extinguish the lamps and put on the gear. The rules and activities for the day are different from the rules and activities for the night, but both serve the same purpose. So, it is with the Old Testament and the New Testament.

People who don't know the difference between night and day think and do all sorts of stupid things because they mix up the rules and activities. Why? Because lost people don't want to live in obedience to God in Christ. They want to do whatever they want to do whenever they want to do it. The secret sauce of faithful understanding is actually wanting for yourself what God wants for you. "You do not have, because you do not ask" (James 4:2).

Do you want to understand the difference between the Old Testament and the New Testament? Or are you just looking for ways to poke holes in Christianity?

Steven: Phillip, you really must get past this notion that a person must believe an idea to understand it. You and I both understand many things that we do not believe. For example, as a Calvinist, I assume you do not believe in transubstantiation, yet as a person who obviously studies religion, I also assume that you fully understand the concept. If you are going to claim that I do not understand the Bible, then it is up to you to explain to me what it is I am missing. You cannot hide behind the idea that I am unable to understand it because I do not hold your beliefs.

Now, it seems as though you are saying that the moral landscape was fundamentally different in Old Testament times than it is now. This doesn't seem to wash with Jesus' clear statement that the old laws must not be changed at all, and that we are to follow them even more strictly than the Pharisees. Either the New Covenant does away with the minutiae of the old laws or it does not. Christ himself seems to indicate plainly that it is the latter. Am I wrong? If so, please refrain from claims that I am not able to understand this because my beliefs are different from yours. Instead, I would welcome your best explanation.

Actually, let me amend my last statement. It seems that in one breath Christ says that we must adhere to the old laws, and in another breath says that we are free to eat whatever we like and to reduce the old laws to a smaller set. It seems clear that this is logically impossible. How do you as a follower of Christ proceed?

Phillip: Christ never says that we are free to do whatever we like. He says that we are free to do what God likes. And God does not want our love to be function of laws. The Lord wants us to want what He wants for us.

Steven: So, is it fair to say that God doesn't want us obeying 600 laws just because he says to and we fear punishment, but rather, that we are to love him and a by product of that love will be following the 600 laws because we love him?

Phillip: Steven, you are so far wrong about this that it isn't funny. Unless Christ's propitiation applies to you personally, you will not make the assumption (an act of faith) that is necessary to understand this issue. You haven't got it yet that the advent of Christ changed things. It would be great to spell it all out in 25 words or less, but life is more complex than that.

The Old Testament laws applied to Old Testament Judaism, which ended in A.D. 70. Even contemporary Israel (even the most fundamental orthodox of the Jews) doesn't do animal sacrifice any more. Things changed. If you don't understand that things changed, that makes you an ultra, narrow-minded, conservative pagan. The Old Testament laws no longer apply in the same way. Most of them have some application or something to teach us about God and faithfulness, but Christians are not obligated to them. 603 of those laws always applied only to Old Testament Jews. The Old Testament Jews did not apply their laws to Gentiles. Ten of them still apply to all humanity, of course, but they apply to those who are in Christ differently than they apply to those who are not in Christ.

Has any of this made a dent yet?

Steven: I suppose we both feel like neither of us is making a dent, though I am honestly trying to understand your position.

You keep hitting me with the same message and I think I've made it clear that I understand you, but it doesn't seem to be sinking in as you regularly accuse me of not getting it. I usually don't do this, but I'm going to raise my voice this once, not in anger, but so that you will hear me.

I UNDERSTAND YOUR POSITION THAT CHRIST'S COMING CHANGED THINGS!

The problem you and I face is the nature of that change. To try to get to the bottom of this, I am going to try and break the issue down and take it step by step by asking you a set of short questions. Hopefully, if we deal with this bit by bit, we will avoid misunderstanding and arrive at the right place.

So, are you now telling me that the 603 Old Testament laws do not apply to the modern Christian, but applied only to the Old Testament Jews of the time, and that the only Old Testament laws that apply to modern Christians are the ten that Moses brought down from the mountain on stone tablets?

Phillip: Steven, Okay, I concede that you understand that Christ has forever changed the world, not just for Christians but for everyone. Now, I am more than willing to press on in the hope that we can find some agreement regarding the nature of the change.

I did not say that the 603 laws have no application to Christians. Here's what I said, "Most of them have some application or something to teach us about God and faithfulness, but Christians are not obligated to them." Do you see the difference between your "reading" of my words and the message that Christians have much to gain by studying those laws regarding the character of God. What is learned by such study provides the application. However, at the same time Christians are not obligated to strict obedience to them, nor to the consequences of disobedience. Yet, Christians will find new ways to please God by discerning modified applications of some Old Testament laws in the light of Christ.

For example: the Old Testament admonitions regarding clean and unclean foods have been rescinded by Christ. Nonetheless, some foods are still better than other foods for a variety of reasons. So, in spite of the fact that all food is now ritually "clean," does not mean that people should not watch their diets. But because metabolism is not identical for all people, we should not make hard and fast rules regarding food.

Regarding the Ten Commandments, I did not say that they "apply to modern Christians." Rather, I said that they apply to all people forever because God's covenant applies to all people forever. And further, they apply to Christians differently than they apply to non-Christians. How so? Christ paid the price for failure to obey them perfectly, but only for those who are in Christ (Christians). Everyone else is still under Old Testament jurisdiction. Another way to say it is that Christ is the lawyer for Christians, but non-Christians must face the Judge with their own resources. Another way is that God has forgiven the trespasses on the basis of Christ's perfect obedience for those who follow Christ. Everyone else remains unforgiven for Adam's sin and for all of their own sins as well.

The difference between these categories of people (Christians and non-Christians) seems to continue to escape your awareness. So, let's try this: before you respond to what I have said, repeat my position in your own words and to my satisfaction, so that both you and I agree that you understand me. Once you understand what I have actually said, then reply. (Yelling is usually an effort to intimidate a person into submission because one's argument has calcified or come to the end of its tether.)

Steven: Active listening! I like it! I will do my best to repeat your position. Please tell me if I have gotten it right. I have some of the words of your statement quoted in an effort to ensure that I am not going astray.

Christians are not obligated to follow all of the 603 laws of the Old Testament, nor are they to suffer the punishments proscribed by God in the Old Testament for breaking them. Rather, most of them have some relevance to their lives and can teach us quite a lot about the character of God. Christians will find "new ways" to please God with "modified" applications of "some" of the Old Testament laws when viewed in the context of Christ's revelation.

Differently, the Ten Commandments apply not only to Christians, but to all people because God's covenant was not just with his chosen people but with "all people forever." Their application to Christians is different from their application to non-Christians because Christ "paid the price" for Christians, but not so for non-Christians (presumably because they have not accepted Christ, but they certainly could). As such, all non-Christians are fully bound by the Ten Commandments, their restrictions and penalties. This is because Christ in his sacrifice of his own life, acts as the Christians' "lawyer" ensuring that they escape judgment. He can do this because he was "perfectly obedient" while we humans are not and probably cannot be.

How did I do?

Phillip: Good. Now reply.

Steven: Well, I suppose my first question would be how do you decide which of the 603 laws have some relevance to your life and which have none at all? Upon what basis are the others disregarded? Second, if the Ten Commandments and the associated punishments for not adhering to them apply to non-Christians, then shouldn't all non-Christians be put to death for breaking the First Commandment? Such punishment is repeated over and over in the Bible. Yahweh is a selfish God and those who do not worship him above all others are to be killed. Finally, how do you reconcile disregarding some of the Old Testament laws and modifying the application of the rest with Jesus' clear statement that we are to adhere to all of the Old Testament law more vigilantly than the Pharisees and that we are not to change a jot or tittle of them?

I like the convention you have established that both of us should repeat the other's statement in our own words to ensure that there is no misunderstanding. Will you please repeat my questions in your own words before responding?

Phillip: Steven, you are asking how Christians can pick and choose various laws to agree with and others to disagree with. What right or basis do they have to do this?

You are also asking, since the Ten Commandments apply to everyone, if non-Christians should be put to death because of their violation of the First Commandment, seeing such instructions in the Old Testament.

And finally, how can Christians disregard some biblical laws in the light of Jesus' instructions to not change a jot or tiddle of the law, and to exceed the righteousness of the Pharisees.

Steven: Very close. I just want to be clear that when Jesus refers to the "righteousness of the Pharisees" he is specifically referring to the 603 laws. The verse right before the "righteousness of the Pharisees" is Matthew 5:19. It says "Whosoever therefore shall break one of these least commandments, and shall teach men to do so, he shall be called least in the kingdom of heaven: but whosoever shall do and teach them, the same shall be called great in the kingdom of heaven."

OK. Good enough. What say you?

Phillip: Steven, I appreciate your questions and sense that they are genuine concerns for you, as they should be for all Christians. I will try to briefly respond to each question with similar concern.

How do we know which laws have relevance and which don't? In a very real sense this is the central question that Christianity needs to deal with more seriously and carefully than it has in the past. The bad news is that it is a huge issue and has not been carefully answered. The good news is that it currently lies at our door and needs to be answered. The first thing to say is that this question cannot be asked before a thorough study of Old Testament law has been made. Part of that study must include the determination of how the light of Christ illuminates each law or issue, or how each law/issue is changed by the light of Christ. After, and not before, these things have been determined can your question be answered satisfactorily.

The basis for disregarding various laws usually involves Christ's fulfillment of Old Testament prophecy. There are several categories of law to consider, i.e., moral law, ceremonial law, cultural law, etc. For instance, Christ's self-sacrifice as the Lamb of God for the sin of the world put an end to animal sacrifice.

Breaking the First Commandment: Should Gentiles be put to death for the transgression of it? Yes and no. Pardon my vacillation, but this is more complex than you might imagine. And the concern of who has jurisdiction to put violators to death is also quite important. The First Commandment in its original presentation has no death demand as a consequence, probably because the death demand for Adam's original sin was still in effect for all of humanity. So, sinners who ignore the First Commandment are already under God's curse which will result in death. All other Old Testament allusions to the First Commandment apply to Old Testament Israel, who officially, legally, verbally covenanted with God to be His people.

The Jews in Jesus' day put Him to death because they thought that He was in violation of the First Commandment because He claimed to be God. Were they correct in that judgment? No. They had forgotten the reality of the Trinity, which is foreshadowed in the Old Testament. When Christ manifested in the flesh as the Second Person of the Trinity, He revealed and fulfilled the reality of one God in three Persons. And that then also means that the First Commandment in the light of Christ now means that the only God worthy of worship is Yahweh Elohim, who is the Father, Son and Holy Spirit. And what is more, eternal life is life in Christ.

So, those who are not in Christ do not have eternal life, and are therefore already condemned to death. However, neither church nor state are given the authority to execute anyone for violation of the First Commandment. Rather, that power is reserved for God Himself, who will exercise His jurisdiction at judgment. In the meantime, Christians are charged with sharing the gospel with everyone and erring on the side of God's grace and mercy in the hope and expectation that God is far more graceful and merciful than any of his people.

Your statement that "Yahweh is a selfish God and those who do not worship him above all others are to be killed" applied to Old Testament Israel. And according to Christianity, Old Testament Israel ended in A.D. 70 with the destruction of the Temple and Jerusalem, which also then ended that law. The Judaism that has survived is not the Judaism of the Old Testament. They no longer do animal sacrifice or kill their kin for worship violations.

Islam has continued it, Christianity has not—BIG difference. So, is Islam in compliance or noncompliance of the First Commandment? Because Yahweh Elohim is Trinitarian, and Islam denies the Trinity—they say the Trinity is God, Jesus, and Mary—and Islam denies the divinity of Jesus Christ, which is required for Him to be the Second Person of the Trinity, Islam does not worship God as Trinitarian. Islam is unitarian. Thus, the God of Islam is not the God of the Old Testament or the New Testament. Nonetheless, Christ did not call for the execution of those who violate the First Commandment. Rather, He calls us to love those who think of themselves as our enemies.

Finally, how can we reconcile Jesus' admonition that "unless your righteousness exceeds that of the scribes and Pharisees, you will never enter the kingdom of heaven" (Matthew 5:20). The scribes and the Pharisees, who were actually very holy by today's standards, had made a wreck of Judaism. The original mission of

Israel was to bring the gospel or blessings of God to the whole world (Genesis 12:3). But by the time that Second Temple Judaism had run its course, the religion of Israel was understood to be the exclusive property of a small, clannish click who struggled to keep God to themselves. This click was represented by the Scribes and the Pharisees. So, Jesus essentially said that Christians had to do better than that!

And what is more, nary a jot or tiddle of the law would change "until all is accomplished" (Matthew 5:18—careful reading is advised). And when would all be accomplished? "When Jesus had received the sour wine, he said, 'It is finished'" (John 19:30). So, it is important that the Old Testament be preserved in tact for a variety of reasons. It provides the context for Christ's advent. It reveals many truths about God's character and about the character of humanity, etc. So, it is to be preserved by not changing a jot or tiddle.

However, now that Christ's redemption has been accomplished/finished, the light of His greater truth shines back on the Old Testament to reveal more than the Old Testament Israelites themselves were able to see. God had veiled the Old Testament Israelites, which Christ then removed. The removal of the veil is an invitation to look again at the Old Testament in the light of Christ.

Matthew 5:19 occurs in the midst of Jesus' Sermon on the Mount, which is understood to be the Christian manifesto, full of "new commandments." I put the quotation marks there because none of Jesus' new commandments are actually new. They are only renewed, given new life in Christ. Thus, "these least commandments" refers to his sermon. Again, none of His "new commandments" were actually new, they had been available to the Pharisees. So, He essentially said that Christians needed to do a better job of obedience than did the Pharisees. And Christians can do this by obedience to Jesus' Sermon on the Mount.

Phillip: (After a long pause of several days) Steven, are we still discussing this?

Steven: You didn't ask me anything.

Phillip: Right, I was answering your question. The next step in reflective listening is for you to repeat what I said in your own words. Once I agree that you heard what I actually said, we can continue. Perhaps taking one paragraph at time is in order.

Steven: Okay, why the heck not? [Gets ready to be disappointed.]

Your first paragraph reads "How do we know which laws have relevance and which don't? In a very real sense this is the central question that Christianity needs to deal with more seriously and carefully than it has in the past. The bad news is that it is a huge issue and has not been carefully answered. The good news is that it currently lies at our door and calls to be answered. The first thing to say is that this question cannot be asked before a thorough study of Old Testament law has been made. Part of that study must include the determination of how the light of Christ illuminates each law or issue, or how each law/issue is changed by the light of Christ. After, and not before, these things have been determined can your question be answered satisfactorily."

If "each law/issue is changed by the light of Christ" then Christ has changed the law that he said must not be changed. This is a direct contradiction. Either Christ was mistaken when he said the law should not be changed at all, or the law should not change.

Phillip: This is not reflective listening. More than copying and pasting is required. You are jumping the gun.

What I said is: yes (agreeing that you have your finger on a real problem for Christianity). But a generic, one size fits all kind of answer will not work. Rather, each of the laws must be studied, and the light of Christ applied to them. Only then, can your question be adequately addressed. So, we won't be doing all of that here. Nonetheless, I provided an example in the second paragraph. Did you notice it?

You are also too quick to want the Bible to contradict itself. It doesn't do that, though understanding what sometimes appears to be contradictions requires time, effort, and suspension of the desire to prove the Bible wrong. If a person is simply working to prove it wrong, s/he will only accept evidence that proves it wrong. So, that attitude must be held in check temporarily so that other options can be seriously considered. This is where you are stuck. But if you will simply "bracket" your desire to prove Scripture wrong for a bit, you might be able to hear what I'm trying to say.

Before you can say that "Christ was mistaken when he said the law should not be changed at all, or the law should not change," you must correctly understand what He actually said. Matthew 5:18 "For truly, I say to you, until heaven and earth pass away, not an iota, not a dot, will pass from the Law until all is accomplished." Note: you added "at all," implying ever. But Jesus didn't say that.

It's like you are locked into a particular intellectual trajectory, so you twist Jesus' words to come out as you expect.

Steven: Phillip, I do not have a burning desire to find contradictions in the Bible. I read it like I would read any other book and many, many contradictions present themselves. Am I to ignore them? On the other hand, you have an ax to grind. You start out with the assertion that the Bible is God's perfect word. Then, when presented with a contradiction, you do back flips to claim that it is not really a contradiction.

A Collision of Belief and Unbelief

The changing/unchanging law represents only a tiny fraction of the assertions in the Bible that contradict each other. Some are ephemeral (God is all powerful, all loving, and yet evil is real and alive in the world today) and some are just statements of events that transpired (Jesus' final words or who he first appeared to after his resurrection). A great many of them simply contradict the observed physical world as we continue to gain a greater understanding of it (water does not transmute into wine and people who have been dead long enough to stink from decomposition are not brought back to life). It is you who is predisposed to making the Bible fit your assumption. Not me.

By the way, to head you off, when I say I "read it like any other book," I mean that I read it in the historical context in which it was written. Unlike many Christians I have encountered who read it like it was written yesterday in their hometown, I understand that it is an ancient anthology and I understand it's historicity.

Phillip: Are we done with the reflective listening thing and back to accusations?

Actually, you are reading the Bible in light of your college education, which issues from the philosophy of the Enlightenment. I have been where you are regarding contradictions and the Bible. And I have never been a Fundamentalist. My background and schooling have all been at the most liberal of the universities and seminaries. So, I really do understand what you are saying.

I'll be glad to continue this conversation, but let's take one issue at a time. All you are doing is throwing out judgments—conclusions about what you think the Bible says. Please don't be so judgmental.

And just to be clear: I do indeed have an ax to grind. As long has I have the ax, it makes sense to keep it sharp. However, the ax is not mine. It was given to me—and that makes me want to take even better care of it. This means that I am prejudiced toward

God. I love Him. I suppose I should have confessed this earlier, but then again you already knew it.

Now you can share your prejudice, just so everything is on the table.

Steven: Fair enough. My prejudice is for reason and evidence.

Phillip: Great! Does this include a prejudice for objective truth?

Steven: To some extent, yes. I believe the things we observe in the world exist mind-independently.

Phillip: It seems that we agree on reason, evidence, and objective truth, though I'm not sure what "mind-independently" means. Which makes our difference to be theological, and your prejudice is against God. Right?

Steven: What God?
And be careful about me and objective truth. Read what I said before you start saying I believe in moral absolutes.

Phillip: As I said, I'm not sure what "mind-independence" is. But as you say, you are blind to God. Are you saying that you absolutely don't believe in moral absolutes? (I put it this way to illustrate a point.)

Steven: Phillip, mind-independence is a way of describing the objective. Something that exists objectively is not dependent on minds to perceive/conceive of it. For example, I perceive my iPad through my senses. The sensations I get from seeing it, hearing it and touching it are all I really know, yet I believe there is an actual iPad there and that my senses are acting upon this objectively real thing. I believe that, even if I did not sense it, it would still exist. I believe this because inductive reasoning shows me that it behaves in predicable ways and because I observe that other people acknowledge its existence and communicate the same or at least very similar perceptions about it that I have.

As to being "blind to God," how do you know there is such a God to which I am blind? What made you decide that such a God exists?

Phillip: Steven, Thank you. Let me first understand what you have said about your Ipad: you have an experience of it that is both visual and tactile. And your only experience of the Ipad is visual and tactile. And from that experience you conclude that there is something to the Ipad that is not dependent upon your senses. It has an "objective" reality that is independent of your senses. Even though all you can really know is sense data, you induce or deduce the existence of a reality (or an aspect of reality) that is beyond your senses, beyond your ability to experience. This concludes my reflective listening, and I'll move on to an analysis of your position.

Note that your example in our discussion about God employs an Ipad, as if the experience of God and the experience of an Ipad are similar or analogous. This comparison insists or implies not simply that God must be material in order to be real, but that God's reality is dependent upon your senses, such that if you personally do not touch, taste, smell, see, or hear God, He cannot be real. In essence, this is the position of a materialist.

From Wikipedia: "In philosophy, the theory of materialism holds that the only thing that exists is matter; that all things are composed of material and all phenomena (including consciousness) are the result of material interactions. In other words, matter is the only substance."

First, this is a very narrow-minded view of reality. It is essentially one dimensional. If reality actually is one dimensional, then it is the correct view. But if there is more to reality than matter (let's even throw electromagnetism into the matter category), then materialism falls short.

This gives rise to some questions: Can something exist even though you have never sensed it? If you were a total hermit, would Ipads actually exist? Also, can your senses sense everything that actually exists? Let's expand this and include machines and human inventions that enhance human sensibility, like telescopes and microscopes. Can something exist that is outside of human sensibility, say a black hole? No one has ever seen a black hole; rather they are assumed to exist based upon barely observable phenomena around them.

I don't want to make this too long, so I'll stop here.

Steven: Materialism is an appropriate term for my world view, yes. I challenge you to defend your claim that it is narrow, though. What makes you think so? Also, magnetism is observable and so falls squarely in materialism.

Can something exist even though I have never sensed it? Yes, but I could have absolutely no knowledge about such a thing. There are hermits and iPads do exist, yes. Machines that expand our senses expand our ability to perceive the universe. Your description of black holes is right on. We do not perceive them directly, and we only posit their existence because of evidence we observe. We do not fully understand them, but that does not mean that we never will. Even if we never will be able to understand them, the questions about them are properly scientific ones.

Phillip: Steven, Okay, it seems that I am doing the reflective listening thing satisfactorily. However, my experience tells me that you are not.

Question: Is there anything non-material that you are able to experience?

Observation: you believe in black holes, even though you (nor anyone else) has ever experienced one. Because you have never sensed one, you "have absolutely no knowledge about such

a thing." The experience from which black holes are posited is not experience of black holes. Right?
This means that black holes are not available for scientific research. Rather, science "posits" ("Posit: [logic] a proposition that is accepted as true in order to provide a basis for logical reasoning") black holes as a theory to explain some other evidence. Black holes are a theory, an idea. Yet, you believe that they are real. Right?
If my logic is flawed somewhere, please let me know.

Steven: Phillip, you are stating that, since black holes have not been observed directly, they do not fall into the material universe and so we can have no knowledge about them. As such, they cannot be studied scientifically. You then ask if there is a flaw in your logic.
Yes, there is a flaw in your logic. Black holes manifest in the physical world. We can observe, measure and study their characteristics. There is evidence that they do indeed exist. As such, they are well within the pursuit of science and, as you should know, are being studied with the scientific method today.
By the way, my use of the word "posit" was incorrect. We hypothesize that black holes exist and the physical evidence to date has confirmed that hypothesis.

Phillip: Steven, Kindly do the reflective listening thing. It will help.
I'm not stating anything now. I'm simply reflecting what you have said. Note how you twist my words to suit your worldview. I did not say that because "black holes have not been observed directly, they do not fall into the material universe and so we can have no knowledge about them."
I agreed with you: "Can something exist even though I have never sensed it? Yes, but I could have absolutely no knowledge about such a thing." Here you said that people can have no

knowledge about something that they cannot experience. This is what you said. To date I have neither agreed nor disagreed.

Then you said, "We do not perceive them (black holes) directly, and we only posit their existence because of evidence we observe." That evidence, however, is not evidence of black holes because, as you have said, we don't perceive them. Scientists perceive information around black holes and hypothesize ("Hypothesize: To believe especially on uncertain or tentative grounds") about them. Note that whether they posit or hypothesize they are devising a theory.

Science is the "study of the physical and natural world using theoretical models and data from experiments or observation." Scientists don't have any data, experiments, or observations about black holes. Rather, they have "holes" in the observable data and posit the existence of something (black holes) that might account for the aberrations in the data. At best black holes are theoretical models.

Question: are those theoretical models called black holes real? Do they actually exist?

Steven: Phillip, you said "Steven, Kindly do the reflective listening thing. It will help." I thought I did! I repeated back what you said in my own words. That's what we're doing, right?

So, after your summary of my post, you stated that science is the study of the material world using models and data from empirical observations. You then said that scientists don't have empirical data on black holes per se, but only unexplained observations for which a hypothesized "black hole" theory might account. You then say that black holes are, at best, theoretical models. Right?

So, I think you have stated this very well. Science does indeed look at empirically observable data and try to account for it with models (hypotheses). They then test those models through experimentation where possible. In the case of black holes, the "experiments" are mathematical models that are adjusted until they fit the data. When hypothesis-testing confirms a particular model, it becomes a supported theory like the atomic theory of matter or the germ theory of disease. This process is, by far, the best method of understanding the world that has ever been devised.

Phillip: Steven, yes, you have summed up what I said very well.
So we sort of agree about how science works. However, you still have not acknowledged that science has no direct, experiential knowledge about black holes. Rather, they have a theory about them that seems to conform to various mathematical models. They have evidence of the surrounding space, not the black holes. Nonetheless, the surrounding space seems to indicate something that conforms to the theory of black holes.

My point, listen carefully for it, is that there is no direct experience or scientific data available for black holes. Right? There is only indirect experience (mathematical data) of the surrounding areas that suggest the veracity of the theory of black holes.

Yet, in spite of this lack of experience or data people believe in black holes. Do you believe in black holes? Are black holes "material," as in your worldview of materialism? And while I'm asking, is math real? Is math part of the material universe?

Steven: Phillip, some things are readily available in the present for scientific study in and of themselves. Viruses, human behavior, and at-hand chemical substances all are good examples of this. Things that are not right at hand, such as the stars because of distance and long-extinct life forms because of time, are studied indirectly through the same methods we use for things that are at hand.

A good analogy is the way we study a murder that has taken place. We cannot directly study the event itself because it has already passed. So what do we do? We collect and analyze empirical evidence. Astrophysicists and evolutionary biologists are like detectives who look at the evidence and form hypotheses to explain it. John Doe's fingerprints were at the crime scene, he was in possession of a weapon that evidence shows was the murder weapon, and he collected $300,000 in life insurance after his wife's death. From this and other forensic evidence, we can conclude with a degree of certainty that he killed his wife. Some cases are stronger than others.

The data that astrophysicists have collected points to something in the physical universe with specific properties, and they have called the explanatory model a "black hole."

You said that you and I have reached agreement on how science works, but said that I still have not agreed that science has no "direct experiential knowledge" about black holes. You then again make the assertion that there is no "direct experience or scientific data" available for black holes. You say that the data collected is only data about the surrounding space. You then say that people believe in black holes in spite of this "lack of experience" of black holes.

Next you ask if black holes are "material" according to my view of materialism. Then you ask if math is part of the material universe. Right?

To answer, I would challenge you to define what "direct experiential knowledge" is. Remember, my view of materialism is that there are actual things out there, even though I can only access by sense data. According to your line of thinking, I do not "directly experience" my dog Bear, because the only data I have are the electrical impulses sent to my brain from my sense organs. I only know about the light reflected off of him, the particles he sheds that hit my olfactory nerves, the vibrations in the air that emanate from him and resound in my ear canal and the varying resistance provided when I place my hand on him. If I understand you correctly, this is not direct experience of him, but only my perception of data emanating from him. To me this is no different from my experience of the data emanating from a black hole, though we have less of it and must use sophisticated instruments to have access to it at all.

As for math, yes, it exists in the material world. Math is a human construct used for understanding the world around us and exists squarely in the neural and chemical complexity of our human brains.

Phillip: Steven, direct experiential knowledge comes through the senses: sight, taste, touch, smell, and hearing. And I posit that you have no direct sense experience of black holes, but much such data directly from your dog, Bear. You can see him, taste him (ick), touch him, smell him, and hear him. You can do nothing of the sort with a black hole. As to whether your sense data provides an experience of Bear's essence, I would say that Bear's dogness is available to your senses. What you sense conforms to the definition of a dog. As to whether your sense data related to Bear provides experience of Bear's "personality" (or "dogality," since dogs aren't persons, which a lot of dog owners will argue against!), I would say that Bear's personality is directly available to you as well. Not so for a black hole.

When you speak of math existing in the material world because it is related to brain function, you are stretching the meaning out of the word "material." On the same logic, I can claim that God exists as a brain function because a lot of people have ideas about Him. In fact, God is one of the most consistent ideas in history, in that every society in history posits a god. He is certainly as real as math.

I'm just trying to show you that both God and black holes can be thought of as being posited or hypothesized to explain various experiential data. Black holes are the theory that seems to best conform to various mathematical modeling and stargazing. There seems to be evidence, not of black holes in themselves, but of the effects that black holes create on the surrounding space. And so it is with God, as well. Yet, you embrace one and reject the other. But enough with the black holes!

Similarly, the historic, biblical, Trinitarian God in Christ is the theory that best conforms to the almost unanimous religious experience of humanity. I'm not saying that all religionists agree about this. I'm saying that the historic, biblical, Trinitarian God in Christ best fits a scientific understanding of religion and the data and experience of religion. There is much religious evidence available throughout history and contemporary social experience across the world.

I will agree with you that almost all the explanations that religionists provide about God are crazy and at best poorly informed and uneducated about the world from a genuine scientific perspective. But that does not mean that the theory of the historic, biblical, Trinitarian God in Christ is wrong, or that God is not real. It just means that there is much ignorance, and much education that needs to happen. I would include you among that group because you also don't appear to know much about the historic, biblical, Trinitarian God in Christ. In other words, you have not sufficiently studied the data, the evidence—the Bible, history, and theology. Science functions as a religion for you.

Let me suggest that the idea of God functions as a kind of axiom: "An axiom is any mathematical statement that serves as a starting point from which other statements are logically derived. Unlike theorems, axioms (unless redundant) cannot be derived by principles of deduction, nor are they demonstrable by mathematical proofs, simply because they are starting points; there is nothing else from which they logically follow (otherwise they would be classified as theorems)." In other words, when God is assumed certain other things can be readily explained.

Why am I thinking that you are not married?

Steven: Very meaty response, and I feel like we are finally getting somewhere. I will need some time to compose a proper response with active listening. I will say now, however, that I would like to pursue your idea that an actual God as described by the Bible and the Christian doctrine of the Trinity is the best explanation of the existence of religion in human culture. I am also interested in your statement that such a God has other explanatory power. I'll compose a formal response later as I am able.

Phillip: I eagerly await your response.

Steven: By the way, I am really enjoying our conversation, particularly our last several exchanges where we seem to be finding common ground and digging into very interesting questions. I still think there is a very large difference between our world views (stating the obvious), but the exchange is stimulating and in a positive way, for me anyway.

Phillip: I agree on all counts—common ground, yet much divergence. In fact, that is the essence of Trinitarian unity, three in one, one in three, diversity in unity, unity in diversity. God Himself is a complex being, yet simple.
You might be interested in *Notes from the Tilt-a-Whirl: Breathing Characters and Talking Rocks,* by N. D. Wilson

Steven: Phillip, I think your distinction of direct vs. indirect experience is an unimportant distraction here and one that has little meaning. In both the case of black holes and pet dogs, we receive empirical sense data about them. My dog barks. A black hole bends light. In both cases, we seek to understand the thing that produces that sense data by examining the data. For me to say that the bent light from the black hole and the air vibrations from my dog are not really the things themselves is not the point. For me to understand them, I observe the data about them. I see little value in claiming that, in examining that data, I am not really examining them.
You also said "When you speak of math existing in the material world because it is related to brain function, you are stretching the meaning out of the word 'material.' On the same logic, I

can claim that God exists as a brain function because a lot of people have ideas about Him."

The fact that our thoughts are actually chemical reactions in the brain is not "stretching the meaning out of the word 'material.'" It is part and parcel of a monistic, materialistic world view and it has much evidence to support it. When the brain is damaged, memories go away, personalities change and emotions are affected. I don't think that our ideas and mental constructs exist in some ether region outside of our brains. Why would I? All evidence points to them existing inside and as part of our brains. In that sense, the idea of God exists squarely in our gray matter as does our mental construct of mathematics. That mathematics seems to work when applied to the real world does not change the fact that it exists in our brains. Do you think it exists somewhere else?

You then, most interestingly, said "I'm just trying to show you that both God and black holes can be thought of as being posited or hypothesized to explain various experiential data." You then claim, "the historic, biblical, Trinitarian God in Christ is the theory that best conforms to the almost unanimous religious experience of humanity."

This is where I think you are wrong. People throughout recorded history have believed in different forms of a supernatural intelligence. Often, they believe that this intelligence intervenes in the physical world. However, the Gods proposed are varied and different in significant ways from the God conception you have. As you know, many of these worldviews posited not one but on many gods. Others posited Gods that are not compatible with the Christian God of which you speak. Also, there is no shortage of explanations for the existence of religion that are far more plausible than the actual existence of such a being.

The evolutionary by-product theory presented by Dawkins makes good sense. Michael Shermer has done excellent work in understanding why people believe and I should not have to say that none of his theories involve God actually existing. Add to this that almost every conception of a monotheistic God entails a logical impossibility, and you can see that God's explanatory value is low, adding more questions than explanations.

Furthermore, a scientific hypothesis is always testable. How would you go about scientific testing to determine if God exists? In the end, this whole line of reasoning is weak to say the least. In the end, you are saying that God exists because lots of people think he does.

I also disagree with your last assertion that God should be presumed as an explanatory axiom. You say "when God is assumed certain other things can be readily explained." I am curious what you think this will explain. I still contend that the actual existence of a logically impossible being is a poor explanation for the fact that humans have asserted the existence of one for millennia.

Finally, to correct a conception you have repeated a few times about me, you said "you also don't appear to know much about the historic, biblical, Trinitarian God in Christ. In other words, you have not sufficiently studied the data, the evidence—the Bible, history and theology." Phillip, my bachelor's degree is in philosophy. I attended Christian college with the intent to become a minister. For the first two years of my graduate education I studied biblical hermeneutics, Koine Greek, religious history, Hebrew, and various classes on Christian theology. Disagreeing with your beliefs does not make me ignorant of them.

Phillip: Steven, you are conflating direct and indirect experience. In fact, no one has any direct experience of light bending. Rather, the experience of black holes is indirect because the black hole is nothing more than a theoretical construct suggested from data readouts from computers. There is nothing at all direct about it. But the dog is immediately before you. What you have said is actually poor science, and I expect that you know better but are so concerned to prove me wrong that you will justify anything in the process—as long as I come out wrong.

Your monistic, materialistic world view serves like a blender to a cup of mixed fruit. At the atomic level you suggest that the fruit is the same before and after blending. But is it? Are not some very subtle molecular relationships changed in the blending process? To him who only has a hammer, everything is a nail. What you are doing in this paragraph is exactly what I accuse you of doing—but you don't see it. So you just roll over it with your monistic steam roller.

It is true that chemistry is involved in brain activity. But is that all that is involved? And is the chemistry the primary cause or a secondary result? Is the chemical reaction the cause of the thoughts? Or are the thoughts the cause of the chemical reactions? Not even the best scientists claim to know this. Are you also instructing them? Again, you overstate your case in the effort to make me wrong, which appears to be your guiding principle.

You provide no evidence whatsoever that you know anything about the historic, biblical, Trinitarian God in Christ or the theology that establishes His reality, yet you think it is wrong. Are you not convinced that it is wrong a priori?[4] Then you suggest that all religious theories are of equal value, which you yourself don't believe. But you are willing to use it in your effort to prove me wrong, regardless of any evidence I suggest. You cite atheistic scholars as if they are "objective" in their analysis, but they are not. Like you, they begin with an assumption and work to establish it as fact. I am not defending or describing a monotheistic god. In addition, I will say again that the god that they (and you) don't believe in is not the God that I believe in. In other words, you are proving that false gods are false. Hey, I agree!

---

4   *A Priori* knowledge or justification is independent of experience, as with mathematics (2+2=4), tautologies (e.g., all bachelors are unmarried), and deduction from pure reason (e.g., ontological proofs). In contrast, *a posteriori* knowledge or justification is dependent on experience or empirical evidence, as with most aspects of science and personal knowledge.

You said that "a scientific hypothesis is always testable." But there are no tests that have or can be run on black holes. The only thing tested is computer modeling and mathematical theories—NOT black holes. But no matter how often or how loudly I say this, you simply dismiss it. Please find an astrophysicist and ask about this.

I am saying that the idea of God is axiomatic, look it up. You might find this article on Set Theory[5] interesting and applicable. I am not saying that God exists because people think He does. I'm saying that there is something to the fact that every culture on earth has posited some sort of god. I'm also agreeing with you that nearly all of their explanations are nonsense. Listen to your language: "I still contend that the actual existence of a logically impossible being ..." In these few words, you have defined this being as a non-existent logical impossibility simply with your adjectives. No serious scientist would do such a thing. Therefore, your analysis is not serious and it is even much less science.

I also have a degree in philosophy, and an M. Div. from the most liberal seminary in the U.S. However, your education has shown what the Bible actually teaches: that Christian belief is not a function of study, intelligence, academics, and especially not philosophy. It is a gift of God. The thing that you cannot understand is that my beliefs are not based upon my degrees or studies —or any sort of proof, logical or other. In fact, Paul particularly warns against the dangers of philosophy (Corinthians I & 2).[6] I have taken that admonition seriously and have not based my theology on it. There is a way out of your confusion, but you gotta wanna. And apparently you don't.

---

5   https://en.wikipedia.org/wiki/Paradoxes_of_set_theory
6   See *Arsy Varsy—Reclaiming The Gospel in First Corinthians*, 2008 and *Varsy Arsy—Proclaiming The Gospel in Second Corinthians*, by Phillip A. Ross, Pilgrim Platform, Marietta, Ohio, 2009.

Steven: Why do think that this line of reasoning only applies to Gnosticism.[7] It clearly attacks modern Calvinist conceptions of God as well.

Phillip: Clearly, you don't know the difference between biblical religion and Gnosticism—neither did the Gnostics. Calvin is most certainly enjoying a good laugh with the Lord at the paucity of the effort to do away with Him. Your view shows itself to provide the foundation of your philosophy, which might be called rational humanism because it rationalizes your desire to escape responsibility for your sin through denial. Denial is a very powerful psychological phenomenon. It is what Scripture calls blindness. And it particularly effects those who over rely on the various ideas of monism. Monists are reductionists who suffer from a kind of one-eyed myopia. In contrast, real Christians are Trinitarian.

Your tendency and temptation will be to yield to your habit of philosophical monism by steam rolling or flattening out the texture of Trinitarianism by reverting to the various historic philosophical treatments of the classic doctrine of the Trinity that devolve into either mystical goo or charismatic abuse. The result is usually either abstractionism[8] or experiential solipsism.

But, truth be told, you are not arguing against the God of the Bible, you are arguing against the gods of your imagination. And like arguing with the straw man, you have proven yourself to be their superior.

---

7   Gnosticism: A modern term categorizing several ancient religions whose adherents shunned the material world and embraced the spiritual world. Gnostic ideas influenced many ancient religions that teach that knowledge, enlightenment, salvation, emancipation, or oneness with God may be reached by practicing philanthropy to the point of personal poverty, sexual abstinence, and diligently searching for wisdom by helping others.
8   Abstractionism: The doctrine that ideas or abstractions actually exist, as in idealism and Platonism. In epistemology, it is the view that knowledge is gained only through abstraction from particulars, and is more commonly called *conceptualism*. It is a kind of philosophical gnosticism.

So, what does your wife think of all of this?

I know so much about you philosophically, it almost seems like we are becoming friends. I have already shared more deeply with you than with many of my friends (only because you operate at a deeper level than most people, and I like that). In addition, one's marriage says a lot about a person. My wife, Stephanie, and I have been married for 25 years. We have three adult sons. We both work from home. You?

(In a private message Steven asked me not to ask about his wife or family again.)

Steven: Please explain why your use of the word "person" for God somehow causes him to not be affected by the arguments presented in my view. It seems as though you are saying that these arguments don't apply to God because he actually exists whereas my view proves he does not. Unless I'm missing something, this has to be the weakest argument I have ever heard.

It is as if I claimed that I was in possession of a proper triangle whose internal angles added up to 360 degrees, and you told me that such a triangle could not possibly exist. Perhaps you even worked through the proof that the internal angles of a triangle must add up to 180 degrees, clear and irrefutable proof that the triangle I claimed to have could not possibly exist. But I say, quite smugly by the way, that this proof only applies to imaginary impossible triangles, not real impossible triangles, and MY triangle actually exists.

So, is that what you are saying?

Phillip: Indeed, you are missing something. I previously called it a blindness. Do you believe you are blind to God's existence? 1 Cor. 1:27 "But God chose what is foolish in the world to shame the wise; God chose what is weak in the world to shame the strong."

The Personhood of God is precisely what you fail to "get." Nor am I able to provide an abstract description of a person for you to logically de-straw. Rather, since you yourself are a person you should be able to provide a logical description for yourself. So, kindly do so. What is a person? In what way are persons different from triangles? I'm not arguing for the logical existence of a triangle, but since that is your concern, please provide a defense for the logical existence of a triangle, and I'll de-straw it.

Steven: Phillip, I guess the active listening thing is over on your part, too.

You keep making assumptions about my motives that are unjustified. My goal is not to prove you wrong. This is not about Phillip to me. My goal is to express clearly to you what my worldview is and why. If I disagree with something you have said, I will dispute it. What else do you expect me to do?

I am indeed saying that any empirical data, whether "direct" or not can be studied with the scientific method to gain knowledge. This whole hair-splitting exercise with black holes is so silly and desperate. We have found anomalous data in the universe, have hypothesized causes for it and tested them with mathematical models. That is science. We assert the existence of black holes to the extent that the model is confirmed by the data and the calculations have been replicated by multiple researchers over time. As our instruments that search the universe improve, we can make predictions about what new data they will provide from black holes based on the model. If the predictions are wrong, then the model will change.

I did not understand what you were trying to say in your paragraph on monism and the fruit smoothie. As for brain chemistry being caused by something else, what is your evidence to support this claim? Is there a reason to think that something else is involved?

You keep saying that I know nothing about your God, so I'd like to learn. Please tell me about him. Does he affect the physical world? Is he good? Evil? Is he good? Is he all-powerful? All-knowing?

Phillip: What is a person?

Steven: An individual human.

Phillip: That raises two questions: 1) what do you mean by "individual"? In what sense are human beings "individuals." 2) Are you familiar with the Corporate Person Controversy? Google it. Why? Because according to U.S. law, corporations are persons, too? With that in mind, What is a person?

Steven: An individual human. We will save a lot of time on these "what does this word mean" tangents if you will use an American English dictionary. As an English speaker, you can assume I agree with its definitions.

Please look up human, individual and person in the dictionary if you are not sure what they mean. I understand that the government treats corporations as individuals for purposes of liability and so forth, but a corporation is not a person. Perhaps this will help clarify.

Phillip: Steven, in fact it is the very definition of a person that is the nub of the issue. You use the dictionary for your definitions, and I use the Bible. I suspect that this accounts for many of our differences. I look to the Bible for the definition and meaning of God, and you look to the dictionary. And here is a significant difference between us: I understand and believe both the dictionary and the Bible, and you understand and believe only the dictionary, but not the Bible. And so you don't see things that are in the Bible because you choose to not believe them.

However, I invite you to examine the human body with the tools of science at the biological or atomic levels in order to see that there are not hard and fast boundaries between individual bodies and/or the environment. Rather, there is much overlapping and interpenetration. This aspect of "person" is suggested in definition 3: "Sociology. an individual human being, especially with reference to his or her social relationships and behavioral patterns as conditioned by the culture." If a person is conditioned by culture, the culture is part of the person in that it contributes significantly to the definition. You might look at the historical definition of the word, as well.

To deny corporate personhood is to deny part of what the Bible defines as the church, which is the body of Christ. As long as you choose to deny the role of the Bible with regard to such definitions and understandings, then we will not come to any significant agreement. However, it is your denial of the Bible in this regard that cuts you off from the deeper, richer, fuller, Trinitarian realities of life provided by God. This is the source of your myopia.

Steven: Phillip, I don't see why your position requires the redefining of certain words. Can you just use other words that more appropriately describe God in mutually well-understood terms? Can't you, as Catholic theologians do, say that God is three persons and one person at the same time (the mystery of the trinity)?

Phillip: Steven, the issue is not my redefining words, but your paucity of understanding regarding language and reality. I'm not redefining words. The Bible is older than the dictionary and functions quite differently. The problem is that you won't accept biblical definitions. The problem, as you have accurately stated it, is that you don't see what I'm talking about. You have a computer programming-like vision of the relationship between language and reality, which does not reflect the context in which we live. The Bible provides the context, the back story that allows us to understand the plot of life more fully.

There is nothing wrong with the three Persons/One Person analogy of the Trinity, except that it is inadequate to portray the texture of the reality of the Trinity. It is not untrue, it is inadequate. That texture is best found in the Bible. Your request reveals a flat, wooden, cold, lifeless understanding. And I understand the draw of such a worldview. It portrays a much easier, less complicated, less confusing world. Everything is cut and dried.

You have obviously spent a lot of time and energy training yourself to boil down complex arguments and aspects of reality in order to extract the essence of their meaning so that you can understand them and arrange them in an order that is meaningful to you. And you have erected quite an impressive structure in the process. But I don't think that you see anything outside of your structure.

And the problem is that when most living things get boiled down, it leaves them dead. The meat is stripped from the bones and the life and color are drained from them in the process. So, you end up with a very neat, analytical construction that is quite precise in its descriptions of the relationships between the various things analyzed. But it's soup.

Your mind is like a blender (I used this analogy earlier), and when you process thoughts you have high, medium and low speeds, but all the speeds do the same thing. Everything gets chopped up into bits for analysis and categorization.

Every piece of textured reality that I try to share with you just gets blended. I hand you a bunch of grapes and you blend them, then ask, "What grapes?"

A lot of people find the books of C.S. Lewis helpful with regard to this sort of concern.

Steven: Phillip, words and their definitions exist so that we may share information and mutual understanding, i.e. communicate. If we cannot agree upon what words mean, then we cannot reasonably communicate. So dictionaries exist to record the definitions of the words we use and serve as a reference for, among other things, resolving disputes about meaning. The Bible, as you know, is a set of books compiled and canonized by the Catholic church.

The books themselves were written in ancient languages on various recovered transcripts. The scholars who translated these manuscripts into Latin, Coptic, English, and a host of other languages used ... wait for it ... dictionaries as one of their set of tools for translation. In fact, the first dictionaries predate the Bible by many years, the first dated at roughly 2300 BCE (the Bible does not predate the dictionary). I understand well that the Bible presents a set of ideas and that you and others view it as ultimately authoritative about the nature of God and the universe. However, the Bible employs language. It does not create it.

As for my world view being "soup," and somehow lacking "meat," I understandably have a different view. The world that science opens up to us is astoundingly large and full of questions yet to be solved. How anyone could look at the natural world and find it lacking in substance and mystery is beyond me. Quite contrary to your view, I think that "soup" more accurately describes your world view. It is chocked full of unjustified assertions, claims that have no evidence, and logically impossible beliefs (that 1 can equal 3 violates the most fundamental rule of logic). So many distractions from the answerable questions in our world.

Phillip: Steven, it is clear that you are a product of your education, which has not taught you anything about Christ—not even your Bible school. Mine didn't either, so I understand the problem.

The crux of the issue is the Person of Jesus Christ and His humanity and divinity co-existing in the individual Person of the Godhead. You're not alone, the vast majority of people are with you. So, in terms of popularity, I'm the oddball. But truth has never been very popular.

Our misunderstanding is not about dictionaries, nor about the meaning of words, nor about the text or historicity of the Bible. It is about Jesus Christ, and who He is. You see Him as a religious teacher born around the year 1 B.C. or A.D. That's the human Christ. But there is another aspect of Christ, which you deny, who is eternal. That Christ is Himself the Word of God to which the words of the Bible point. That Christ gave us language, and nothing was written before He gave us language. Everything issues from and inheres in Him.

The world that can be know through science, large though it is, cannot hold a candle to whole of reality, which can only be truly known through Jesus Christ, the second Person of the Trinity. There is much more to genuine truth than science can demonstrate. God has given us science in order to know Him better.

My "assertions" are neither unjustified nor without evidence. Rather, you deny the justification and the evidence because you don't see it. May I suggest that the Lord has withheld it from you? I hope not, but I don't see any evidence to the contrary.

Nonetheless, to show you some of what you are missing, let me suggest that you look again at Set Theory because Christs are in union with Christ. "Union of the sets A and B, denoted A ∪ B is the set of all objects that are members of A, or B, or both. The union of {1, 2, 3} and {2, 3, 4} is the set {1, 2, 3, 4}." Why do I point to this? Surely, you know of Plato's problem of the one and the many. Christianity solved this problem in the twentieth century.[9] Did you miss it?

To reduce the Trinity to math sucks the life out of it. No one is saying that 1 = 3, that's absurd. However, $1 * 1 * 1 = 1$, and $1 / 1 / 1 = 1$. Even $1^\infty = 1$. The Trinity is about higher orders of existence, which can be analogously known through higher orders of math.

Steven: Phillip, you said "My 'assertions' are neither unjustified nor without evidence. Rather, you deny the justification and the evidence because you don't see it." I have heard this refrain

---

9   See the work of Cornelius Van Til (www.vantil.info) and *The One And The Many: Studies In The Philosophy Of Order And Ultimacy*, by R.J. Rushdoony, Thoburn Press, 1978.

before, that there is indeed compelling evidence for religious claims, but that I and others like me don't recognize them. The problem with this claim is that for something to be evidence it must be "evident." To illustrate, when people understand that no two individuals have the same fingerprint pattern, and the latent fingerprints of someone are found in a particular location (usually a crime scene), it is evident, even to a small child, that the fingerprints are evidence that the person was in that location. No sane person who understands the facts would dispute this, and that evidence is so powerful that we use it to help decide the dire fate of those accused of crimes.

By contrast, I have never learned of "evidence" for the existence of God that is evident at all. Some are a priori arguments that easily fail under the simplest analysis. Some people tell me that mountains and sunsets are evidence for God, but conveniently overlook things like smallpox, pediatric cancer, and the constant, violent, murderous competition among organisms in the natural world. But, I have not heard what you believe to be evidence so I will ask you directly. What is your evidence for your worldview?

Bay the way, the doctrine of the Trinity does indeed say that 3 = 1 and 1 = 3, at least when it comes to God. We can test if your view asserts the same thing if you will answer a few questions.

Is there one God or several?
Is the Father fully God?
Is the Son fully God?
Is the Holy Spirit fully God?

Also, and maybe this will be more truly illustrative of your belief, what is the difference between a being and a person? Is a person a being?

Phillip: Steven, I am giving you such good information, but you ignore it and continue with your same old sorry song that you just don't see God. Nonetheless, I'll show you the evidence you want: Close you eyes. ... Open them. Voila! You, your own life, is the evidence that God exists, as am I. If you don't see it, there is only one reason: you are like the unbelieving Jews.

"But their minds were hardened. For to this day, when they read the old covenant, that same veil remains unlifted, because only through Christ is it taken away" (2 Corinthians 3:14).

"But when one turns to the Lord, the veil is removed" (2 Corinthians 3:16).

So, whether you see or not, you are the evidence you seek. Beyond that, I cannot show you what you refuse to see. You must remove your own veil, your resistance.

However, I agree with you that the god you want me to prove doesn't exist. So, kindly stop asking about such silliness. Your Trinity math is simply wrong because it assumes a logical impossibility. 1 does not equal 3. Trinity math is a higher order math, like multiplication and division, as I said previously. Simple summation doesn't cut it.

Oh, and "smallpox, pediatric cancer and the constant, violent, murderous competition among organisms in the natural world" also provide evidence of God. How? Because you object to them, you don't like them. So, why do you object to them?

Why won't you tell me about your wife? Are you embarrassed or hiding something? I have answered your direct question about providing my evidence for God (in the first paragraph, if you missed it).

Steven: Phillip, ...really? That's your evidence for the existence of a Triune God? That people exist? The fact that we don't know for sure exactly how the first replicating molecules came into existence does not point to supernatural origin, let alone one of the many conceptions of God that have arisen throughout humanity. Again, evidence must be evident. The existence of human beings does not make it evident that a supernatural, Triune God exists.

People cannot be "blind" to true evidence.

Phillip: Steven, Let's come back to this discussion in twenty years. I trust the old adage that time wounds all heels.

Steven: Phillip, the reason that I "object" to pediatric cancer and smallpox is that they are direct causes of immense amounts of human suffering. The reason I don't like human suffering is that, like you, I am a member of a species that has evolved to be compassionate to my fellow humans. That we help each other out when in distress is a clear survival advantage for the species as a whole. It is one of the many reasons that we are the dominant species on the planet.

By the way, science and human compassion, not a triune deity, are what eradicated smallpox, and medical science continues to be the best hope for children with cancer. One must wonder, if God is inherently good and man inherently sinful, why God would ignore diseases that bring a painful, terrifying death to children and mankind is the one who stops them.

Phillip: Again, modern science and medicine owe their origin to Christianity. If it weren't for Christ, no progress would have been made. The "direction" of "evolution," as you have suggested, is into the light, which God provides. Thank you, Jesus!

Steven: The late-to-the-game claim that Christianity is responsible for modern science and medicine is nonsensical. To steal from another author who has explained it in a way that I cannot better:

"… this kind of Christian apologetic argument fails for several reasons which fall into the trap of several fallacies including: appeal to ignorance (failing to understand the history of Christianity in how it did little to inspire science during the Dark Ages); confusing correlation with causation (just because a scientist accepts religion doesn't mean his science derived from religion); and non sequiturs (it doesn't follow that just because a few scientists believed in God that science resulted from it)."

Scientific facts have never derived from religion, but religion has conceded several positions to science, a trend that will continue. Why do you suppose this "we invented science" stance is coming so late to the apologetic game? No apologist worth his salt would have argued this during the Christian Dark Ages or even during the Reformation. Why now? By the way, if you still want to claim that Christianity is responsible for science, please explain how the ancient Greeks and Romans did science before Christ was born.

As for evolution being directed into "the light, which God provides" ... Phillip, you do not understand evolution. Evolution by natural selection, as its name implies, is not directed. It happens naturally without any guiding hand.

Phillip: Again, you are such a product of your government education (read: indoctrination). The fact that unfaithful people argue against God proves only their lack of faith—which neither you nor I would argue against. Honestly, Steven, do you really think that science knows that evolution is not guided? The "just happens naturally" argument is actually the dark box of "we have no idea how it happens." Show us your evidence for this? Point to the experiments that have established this "fact."

Steven: Public education does not "indoctrinate" ideas. It teaches them. It encourages questions and rewards creative thinking. Conversely, religion does depend on childhood indoctrination. It discourages questions and eschews creative thinking. If you doubt this, consider that a person's religion is almost always the religion of their parents. Had you been born and raised in Iran, educated in the ways of Islam and sent daily to a Madrasah, do you think you would be a protestant Christian today?

Yes, we know that evolution is unguided. It happens through natural selection which has been observed and proven. You ask me to "Show us your evidence for this? Point to the experiments that have established this 'fact.'" Happy to do it.

The Lenski experiments are seminal.[10] They take advantage of the fact that microbial generations are much shorter than most, and so we can observe change over time in ways that are not possible with more complex organisms. This is but one of many, many such experiments that prove natural selection. Please read about it.

Phillip: No one disputes species adaptations, also called micro-evolution. It's the species transitions or macro-evolution of the microbes to human beings sort that doesn't appear to happen. So, Lenski found that e-coli adapt to their environments. Correct. But after 50,000 generations they are still e-coli. Adaptation, not evolution—we can argue about semantics some more if you want. This is a common confusion. I expect better from you.

Sometimes I wonder if I'm talking to a person or an algorithm because you can't seem to hear the central point of my concern: that the idea of god that you argue against is not the God I argue for. Are you the same religion as your parents? What is your childhood religious background? Mine is liberalism—UCC. My folks were very active and so was our family.

Steven: Phillip, you do not understand evolution. The organisms we see today did not go through 50,000 generations. They went through millions of generations. It is not possible for us in our short timescales to observe a microbe turn into a plant cell. All evolutionary change is small and cumulative. If you believe in micro evolution, then you believe in evolution. "Micro" is the only evolution that occurs. As for speciation, the evidence for it is

---

10 The E. coli long-term evolution experiment is an ongoing study in experimental evolution led by Richard Lenski that has been tracking genetic changes in twelve initially identical populations of asexual Escherichia coli bacteria since 24 February 1988. The populations reached the milestone of 50,000 generations in February 2010 and 60,000 in April 2014.

overwhelming. We have observed plant gene pools that have been separated by geographic changes into two isolated gene pools and each, adapting to different conditions, has gone down its own evolutionary path. Today, they are incapable of interbreeding. Species are defined as organisms that can interbreed, so we have in these plants a clear example of speciation, and it is not the only one.

I have heard from you several times now the common apologist's refrain that the God I describe is not the God in which you believe. Let's get past this as much as we can by nailing down a few characteristics of your God. Let's start small so that we can make measurable progress toward a common understanding. I should point out that so far, I have asked you questions about your God that should be readily answerable, but have received quite long-winded replies that introduce more questions than answers. I understand that God is a substantially complex topic, yet there are many complex things about which simple questions can be answered simply, albeit with complex implications. For example, a cosmologist can be asked if he or she believes the universe is infinite, and we can expect a yes or no answer to this question, though the explanation of the answer will likely take significantly more words.

So, starting small, is the God you believe in omniscient?

Phillip: Hold the show! "It is not possible for us in our short timescales to observe a microbe turn into a plant cell." No evidence!?

"We have observed plant gene pools that have been separated by geographic changes into two isolated gene pools and each, adapting to different conditions, has gone down its own evolutionary path." We have? I missed that memo. Wait a minute, here it is: "adapting to different conditions." Not macro evolution.

"They went through millions of generations" This is pure speculation. Show me the evidence of this.

Macro evolution is a theory, even a scientific theory—but a theory. Not a fact. There is no evidence. And even if there were something that we would like to label as evidence, that kind of knowledge is not available to our world of discourse. And only unmitigated pride dares to think that it is.

I hear that you have heard that the God I believe is not the god you describe. But the issue here is not about the deity, it's about you. The worldview of unbelievers is not the worldview of believers, by definition. You want to meld them, but they cannot be melded. In part this means that what you understand by omniscient is not what God understands by omniscient. So, if I were to answer "yes" you would think that unbelieving omniscience is the same as believing omniscience, and make another untrue assertion. And if I answer "no" you will find something else to accuse me of.

Steven, I'm beginning to doubt your personhood. Can you prove to me that you are an actual person and not an atheistic algorithm? Seriously.

Steven: Phillip, you cannot have it both ways. You cannot claim that I have an incorrect conception of your God and then obstinately refuse to answer questions about him. Omniscience is a simple concept. Either God knows everything or he does not. Which is it?

And I am a real human being. Ask John. I used to play racketball with him.

Steven: Phillip, the evidence for the age of life on earth is overwhelming and confirmed through multiple methods in multiple disciplines. Geology, genetics, biology ... all support this scientific fact. It is not conjecture.

By the way, do you see the irony here? You assert that your belief was given to you by God and repeatedly make assertions that you have no evidence. Yet, what do you demand of me? Evidence! "Show me the evidence of this," you demand. Even more ironic is that there are mountains of mutually confirming pieces of evidence gathered from different fields of study that confirm all of the things you deny about evolution and not a shred of scientific evidence for your own claims.

But, back to brass tacks. Is the God you believe in omniscient?

Phillip: Steven, Omniscience is not a simple concept. As a student of philosophy you should know this. My concern is not to feed your unbelief by giving you the straw men you want to slay as a show of your superiority to God. To know whether or not God knows everything, we must first have a common understanding of "God," which we don't have. Then we need to understand epistemology,[11] which we have not discussed. And finally we would need to have a common perception of "everything" (the object of knowledge) which we don't have. So, because you and I have so many divergent, fundamental perceptions and beliefs it is doubtful that our use of words includes common definitions, which we know from our conversation that we don't have.

We might begin by discussing whether omniscience (having infinite knowledge) is possible. Why or why not?

The evidence for the age of the earth is derivative and indirect, not direct. All we have are scientific instruments and theories. For instance, Paleontology (the study of fossils) is important in the study of geology. The age of rocks may be determined by the fossils found in them. Yet, at the same time, scientists determine when fossils were formed by finding out the age of the rocks in which they lie. Do you see the circularity here?

"Are the authorities maintaining, on the one hand, that evolution is documented by geology and, on the other that geology is documented by evolution? Isn't this a circular argument?"

---

11 Epistemology: the theory of knowledge, especially with regard to its methods, validity, and scope. Epistemology is the investigation of what distinguishes justified belief from opinion.

(Azar, Larry, "Biologists, Help!," *Bioscience*, vol. 28, 1978, pp. 714.)

"The procession of life was never witnessed, it is inferred. The vertical sequence of fossils is thought to represent a process because the enclosing rocks are interpreted as a process. The rocks do date the fossils, but the fossils date the rocks more accurately. Stratigraphy cannot avoid this kind of reasoning, if it insists on using only temporal concepts, because circularity is inherent in the derivation of time scales." (O'Rourke, J.E., "Pragmatism Versus Materialism in Stratigraphy," *American Journal of Science*, vol. 276, 1976, p. 53).

"Paleontologists cannot operate this way. There is no way simply to look at a fossil and say how old it is unless you know the age of the rocks it comes from. ...And this poses something of a problem: If we date the rocks by the fossils, how can we then turn around and talk about the pattern of evolutionary change through time in the fossil record?" (Eldridge, Niles, *Time Frames*, 1985, p. 52). There's lots more.

I do not assert that my belief was given to me by God. I acknowledge that God has provided an historic revelation of Himself throughout history. The direct evidence is biblical, the indirect evidence comes from theology, history, philosophy, archeology, etc. The personal evidence is how God (my interaction with all of this evidence) has changed my life in the very ways predicted by the Bible. However, my faith is not a product of evidence. It is a presupposition that brings the light of Christ to the evidence so that it can be seen for what it actually is. It provides the best possible historic context for the evidence.

I do not know in order to believe, but rather I believe in order to know. Before you criticize me for this, note that you do the same thing. I "believe" and what I know flows from that belief. You "don't believe" and what you know flows from that unbelief.

You are the one who said that your theological position is based upon evidence. I'm just asking you to show the evidence you claim, in this case about the theory of evolution. Note: you didn't show it, but tried to shift the burden of proof to me.

Steven: Phillip, after refusing to answer as to whether the God you believe in is omniscient, you said. "To know whether or not God knows everything, we must first have a common understanding of 'God,' which we don't have." Please explain how we are to have a common understanding of the God in which you believe when you will not answer some pretty basic theological questions about him. And, bro, relax. I am not asking you about omniscience because I have some grand trap laid for you. Either the God you believe in is omniscient (in whatever way you want to frame it) or he is not. You can only elaborate on a quality of God when you first affirm that God has that quality.

Your attack on the dating of fossils and rocks is ill-informed. Yes, it would be circular reasoning if scientists said, "We measure the age of rocks completely by looking at the fossils near them, and we measure the age of fossils completely by looking at the rocks near them." It should come as a surprise to no one that this is not what happens.

Scientists date rocks using isotope half-lives, as I suspect you know. From this starting point, they can tell the age of fossils found embedded in those rocks. After cataloging many fossilized specimens, we know in which geologic era they lived. Thus, when we find another such specimen in rocks that do not lend themselves to radiometric dating, we can infer the age of the fossils and the rocks in which they are found. Not quite the circular reasoning fallacy you present.

By the way, your insistence that science cannot make such inferences demonstrates a basic ignorance about how science is conducted. According to you, if we can't see something happening right in front of us, we can have no scientific knowledge about it. This would be sad if it were true, since the number of things that happen right in front of us is pretty limited. Also, it would mean an end to the popular "CSI" television series and its scientists who gather and analyze evidence about a crime that often nobody has observed directly. Don't they know that what they're doing isn't really science but just inference?

Scientific inference is one of the best tools human beings have for understanding reality. Your pooh poohing of it is, to be polite, underwhelming.

You also said "I do not assert that my belief was given to me by God." My mistake there, and I apologize for making it. I thought I recalled you espousing the Calvinist doctrine of the elect. I could have sworn that you said that God chooses the saved and not the other way around. If I was mistaken, *mea culpa*.

Finally, your claim that there is no evidence for evolution is, there is no kinder way to put it, laughably ridiculous. When Darwin published *On the Origin of Species* 150 years ago, he had already collected significant amounts of evidence from specimens in the Galapagos that directly supported evolution by natural selection. Since that time, the discovery of genetics confirmed his assertion of inherited traits and provided the mechanism by which it occurs. Fossils, ordered correctly in the geological strata, were discovered in droves, all supporting the idea of evolution by natural selection. (By the way, a single fossil found in the wrong strata would disprove Darwin's theory. It has never happened. Not once.)

Laboratory experiments on drosophila, bacteria and multiple other life forms have confirmed Darwin. His theory made predictions about what naturalists would find in new locations and those predictions held true. Vestigial traits like the recurrent laryngeal nerve are very strong evidence of common ancestry according to Darwin.

I could go on and on, but I shouldn't have to. You should have already been educated about this, but you apparently have not. It is sad. There is still time, though. I urge you to read a good book on evolution that is not written by an author with a creationist agenda. *The Greatest Show on Earth*, by Dawkins will answer most of your recurring questions.

By the way, if belief in God is necessary to understand what God is, how does anyone end up believing in God?

Phillip: Steven, our exchanges are interesting in an odd way. I can't call it communication because, while I think I understand what you are saying, I don't think that you understand what I'm saying. Apparently, you don't see my answer to your question about God's omniscience. You are determined to pound a round God into your square hole, and will accept nothing other than a square god as God. I'm saying that we do not have a common understanding of God and it grows more clear with each exchange that we are not going to. I have chosen not to elaborate on God's omniscience because I know that your flawed understanding of God will pervert your understanding of His omniscience.

Your question, "if belief in God is necessary to understand what God is, how does anyone end up believing in God?" is the very question that you must answer. But you cannot answer it because your whole warp and woof is hopelessly godless. In fact, you have adequately defeated the Arminian view of God. Your concern about election also reveals that you have an Arminian view of Calvinism, as well. How could it be otherwise?

Our communication problems might be happening because God does not treat everyone the same. How so? He treats believers differently than He treats unbelievers. I'd like to help you see things differently, but it seems that you can't hear me.

Steven: 1- Is God omniscient? [Refused to give even a qualified answer.]
Let's try something even smaller. Does God know what will happen in the future?

Phillip: Steven, It is clear to me that this line of inquiry will not get us anywhere. It is not likely that you and I are going to find agreement on anything.

You have discovered that various historic proofs of God are ludicrous. And they are. Because the idea of God functions axiomatically, the idea of God is not susceptible to the kind of proof you seem to want. You seem to think that this fact implies that God, therefore, does not exist. But just because a bunch of monkeys can't do science does not mean that all science is false.

The errors of Christian theology do not necessarily imply anything about God, precisely because they are errors. Falsehoods do nothing for the establishment of truth. A million false statements will never add up to truth. But neither do they necessarily imply that there is no such thing as truth. In fact, the fact that they are false assumes some truth against which they are measured to determine their falsehood. Such things simply expose the errors, sins, and immaturity of those who assert them.

The fact that people misinterpret and/or misunderstand various kinds of scientific data does not mean that the general practice of science is meaningless or foolish. And the same thing applies to God and the Bible. The fact that people misinterpret and/or misunderstand various things about the Bible does not mean that God is not real or that the Bible is not true. It just establishes rather than eradicates the reality of sin.

Can we agree that people are generally ignorant?

Steven: 1- Is God omniscient? [Refused to give even a qualified answer.]
2- Does God know what will happen in the future? [Refused to give even a qualified answer.]
Is God eternal?

Phillip: Are you a sinner?

Steven: 1- Is God omniscient? [Refused to give even a qualified answer.]
2- Does God know what will happen in the future? [Refused to give even a qualified answer.]

3- Is God eternal? [Refused to give even a qualified answer.]
Is God the creator, i.e. did God create the universe and everything in it?

Steven:
1- Is God omniscient? [Refused to give even a qualified answer.]
2- Does God know what will happen in the future? [Refused to give even a qualified answer.]
3- Is God eternal? [Refused to give even a qualified answer.]
4- Is God the creator, i.e. did God create the universe and everything in it? [Silence...]

Phillip, for a Christian minister, you are the most tight-lipped person about God I have ever met, even when people ask you direct questions about him! I will ask you the most softball question a minister could ever get:
What is God?

Phillip:
1- Is God omniscient? God is wiser than you and I are. A better question is: What does God know that I don't know?
2- Does God know what will happen in the future? God has a plan and will complete it. A better question is: What does God think of my future?
3- Is God eternal? God is the longest living being. A better question is: How is God's perspective different than mine?
4- Is God the creator, i.e. did God create the universe and everything in it? As you know, Genesis 1:1-3 says: "In the beginning, God created the heavens and the earth. The earth was without form and void, and darkness was over the face of the deep. And the Spirit of God was hovering over the face of the waters. And God said, 'Let there be light,' and there was light." A better question is: "Where were you when I laid the foundation of the earth? Tell me, if you have understanding." (Job 38:4).

5- What is God? God is real. God is becoming. God said to Moses, "I AM WHO I AM." (Ex. 3:14).

What Bible school did you go to? What is your church background? Do you have children? Have you been baptized? How do you know right from wrong? Are you now or have you ever been an algorithm? Have you ever lied?

Okay. I answered your questions, answer mine.

Steven:

1- Is God omniscient? [Still refuses to answer. Proposes a different question.]

2- Does God know what will happen in the future? [Still refuses to answer. Proposes a different question.]

3- Is God eternal? [Still refuses to answer. Proposes a different question.]

4- Is God the creator, i.e. did God create the universe and everything in it? [Yes.] Holy mackerel! An answer! For perhaps the first time in our conversation together, you have actually said something about the God you believe in! See, if you would do more of this, you could stop complaining that I am not talking about your God.

So, a follow up question for you about this. What is your reason for asserting that God created everything? Is it because it is written so in Genesis?

5- What is God? God is real. God is becoming. God said to Moses, "I AM WHO I AM." (Ex. 3:14).

Another answer! Now we are getting somewhere! When you say that God is "real," what do you mean? Is he in our universe? Does he exist physically? Spiritually? Both? Also, when you say God is "becoming" can you clarify? Does that mean that he is changing, perhaps into a target state?

I did not go to seminary. I was raised Catholic, switched to Southern Baptist in my teens. I was quite active in my church and my Biblical studies. Since then, I have been Presbyterian and Lutheran.

I have talked to you specifically about my family already (by asking me not to ask about it—ed.) and I am surprised you are asking this question.

I was baptized both Catholic as an infant and Southern Baptist in my teens.

I know right from wrong in exactly the same way that you do; by making conscious, entirely personal choices about the moral principles I value and then basing my actions on those principles. The principles themselves have an evolutionary origin (for both of us).

I am a human being, and there is ample evidence for coming to that conclusion. However, if you would like to mistakenly believe something that is not the case, go right ahead. You seem to be good at it [rimshot!] (Sorry, I couldn't resist).

Of course. We have all lied before we could even speak. Mark Twain explains it entertainingly well in his essay, *My First Lie and How I Got Out of It*.

Phillip: Steven, I could be wrong, but it seems that you do not believe in God or Jesus Christ. Do you believe that God is real? That the Bible is true? Do you consider yourself to be a Christian? Are you currently in a spiritual crisis?

If you do not rely upon the Bible for your knowledge of right and wrong, then you don't do it like I do.

By "real" I mean actual, and by "actual" I mean an actor in the world. Jesus Christ is God by the power of the Holy Spirit. God is truth.

What principles have an evolutionary origin? I don't understand this.

Steven: Phillip, I am a skeptic and not in a spiritual crisis. You ask if I believe the Bible is "true," and based on our earlier conversations, I think you would say that I do not. With regard to morality, the Bible has some pretty awful stuff in it; morally repugnant by today's standards. With regard to internal consistency, the Bible does as well as one would expect from an anthology of books whose original transcripts we don't have, and whose texts have been translated and transcribed many, many times over the millennia. In other words, there are many factual inconsistencies in the Bible and it does not impress me as being a source of historical truth.

You say that if I don't rely upon the Bible for my knowledge of right and wrong then I don't do it the way you do, but this is not true. We both select moral principles that make sense to us. People who look to the Bible for their knowledge of right and wrong do so because they themselves have decided that the Bible is God's word; not the Koran, not the Bhagavad Gita, and not their own moral compass. It is you who have decided that the Bible is God's perfect moral instruction and so your decision to follow those moral precepts is totally yours, just like my decision to follow the principle of human well-being is mine. It does no good to say "My rules are God's rules" as though that somehow relieves you of the responsibility of choosing your own moral course.

So, to repeat your own words, you believe that God is "an actor in the world," that He does things that are physical and real.

Our nature to feel empathy and to want to help people who are in distress, even if we don't know them, comes from evolution. Those tribes that felt the pain of their neighbors and worked together to survive were better able to pass those empathy genes on to their offspring.

Phillip: Steven, I would say that a skeptic does not have a settled position, and thus is in some state of spiritual crisis. I don't want to suggest that a spiritual crisis must be some sort of emotional handicap, simply that "crisis" and "skeptic" share a sense of unsettledness.

Regarding your belief in the Bible. For many years I read the Bible as you probably do. Many of its stories and facts don't measure up to our modern experience of how things work. There are indeed many apparent contradictions in the Bible, and they provide serious difficulties. I have studied the liberal literature and have come to at least two conclusions.

First, there are people who study the Bible in order to prove it wrong because they don't believe in it and are psychologically motivated to justify their unbelief. The Bible speaks of this problem a lot. It calls such people by various names: pagans, false teachers, false gods, etc. My point is that such people are not simply a modern phenomenon. While the modern version of unbelievers try to suggest that they are "objective" and "neutral" in their approach to biblical study, they are not. They approach the text as skeptics, bringing doubt and disbelief with them. And they find what they are looking for: contradictions, impossibilities, etc.

Second, there are others who study the Bible in order to prove it right because they believe in it and are spiritually motivated to find justification for their belief. The Bible speaks of such people as believers, faithful, etc. Many (maybe even most) of these modern believers were educated in Enlightenment principles and have failed to understand that there is no such thing as "objective" and "neutral"—especially with regard to God and the Bible. Nonetheless, they have tried to make biblical faith respectable by infusing their studies with with the airs of objectivity. In my opinion, this is the view of God and the Bible that you object to. And, wait for it, ... so do I!

Thus, the thing that you don't and can't understand is that that's not my understanding of God or the Bible, etc. So, your perspective does not threaten my faith because it does not address what I believe. Yes, you want me to define various things about God, but you want to put my perspective into your categories— and it won't work. It's not that I think that you are lying in wait to trap me, but that your categories of understanding are not adequate to what I believe. You want simple "yes" and "no" answers to plug into your categories of analysis. But because I've been there, I don't play that game. If you really want to know what I believe and/or how I understand the Bible, it will require some serious study, and it will require a different attitude or approach to the issue.

You must stop reading the Bible in order to prove how it is wrong, and pretend that you believe it, so you can ask, "How might this story be true?" I'm convinced that we (the modern world of both believers and unbelievers) have mistranslated and misunderstood the Bible in many ways. This began very early—very early. Read Jude. We are reading our assumptions of our own "objectivity" into the translations.

The story of the Bible is not what is commonly thought among believers, and much less among unbelievers. The whole of the larger context is not part of the popular mindset. The fact that people have misunderstood this does not mean that God is a false or that the Bible is wrong. It simply verifies the reality of sin and magnifies the grace of God.

In fact our (yours and mine) different methods for determining good and evil are not alike, though you think they are because you don't and perhaps cannot conceive of any other method. First, it is not that I have decided myself that the Bible is true and therefore I believe it. My personal acknowledgment of its truth comes late in the process and is not a decisive factor. Prior to my acknowledgment, the historic community of Christ (the church) has been living out this truth for a long time, even though there is much misunderstanding, as previously mentioned. Biblical morality is not like brain surgery or nuclear physics. It is not difficult to understand, the difficulty is in the doing. God has imposed and demanded a morality that is beyond our human ability to manifest.

Sure, an individual here and there has excelled now and again, but widespread cultural adaptation has practically never happened, and certainly not in any large populations. It may have been Chesterton who said that Christianity has not been tried and found lacking, but that it has been found difficult and never been seriously tried—socially. To say that America is or was a Christian nation is laughable, though it has perhaps been the most Christianized of the nations. The American experiment has always been a compromised endeavor.

You said that you think that I believe the Bible because I decided to believe it a priori. So, you think that I decided that biblical morality is best, whereas others opt for other versions of morality that are equally valid and defensible. This is the ground for moral relativism, which is your skeptical position. I only ask for you to be consistent by being as skeptical about this as you are about the Bible, God, and biblical morality. For, if your skepticism does not also apply at this point, it is no longer skepticism but atheism because of its commitment to moral relativity and denial of God. I will trust (hope) that you can do this.

While I don't say that my rules are God's rules, I endeavor to say that God's rules are my rules, Lord willing. It is not that "belief" in the Bible absolves me or anyone else of moral responsibility, but rather that the Bible makes human moral responsibility entirely unavoidable. Being a Christian does not reduce personal moral responsibility, it heightens and adds to it. In fact, the Bible defines moral irresponsibility as doing what you say that you do —decide for yourself. Doing what you (or any individual) wants to do cannot be defined as moral responsibility. That kind of approach is actually immoral because morality by definition is conformity to an agreed upon social code of behavior. Christians, the church, agree that human behavior is best engaged according to biblical morality in the light of Christ (don't neglect this last phrase).

Sure, we actually don't do it all that well, but that is the affirmed model. Don't judge biblical morality on the basis of Christian behavior, judge it on Christ's behavior—that's the model. The worst thing about Christianity is the fact that Christians claim it. Christians are the worst possible argument for the reality of Christianity—not because Christianity is not true, but because it can only be manifest inasmuch as one's whole culture manifests it because the heart of Christianity involves the wholeness of humanity. So, apart from that wholeness (which is currently horribly fractured) it isn't yet wholly Christian.

If you want to argue that human empathy comes from the principles of the survival of the fittest, then why not apply that idea to Christianity itself, since Christianity has proven itself to be the fittest of the religions regarding its survival? If we can believe the essence of the biblical creation story, then we can see that God began by instructing Man about how to live in this world. Don't get hung up on the details about how creation happened, or even about exactly what God created. The actual text doesn't go into the detail that we demand of it today. And "the devil is in the details." (I'm just saying that the actual details are not given in Scripture, and that they are dependent upon speculation. They are not essential to the story at this point.)

God instructed humanity, and humanity didn't follow God's instructions. Yoel Natan argues decisively in his book, *The Jewish Trinity*, that Yahweh Elohim is Trinitarian. Thus, Christianity broadly conceived has always been the heart of the biblical story. This means that God's instructions for humanity are perfected in Jesus Christ. What Christ taught has always been the intention and teaching of God and His Bible. So, what you call evolutionary empathy for the fellowship of humanity (if I may use that phrase) originated from God. And has been a kind of evolutionary process (in the sense of micro adaptations) as humanity has grown and matured as a species. (Though evolution cannot bring humanity to the fulfillment of the process, which requires a new creation as discussed in Revelation. But that's another tangent.)

Steven: Phillip, you said, "a skeptic does not have a settled position, and thus is in some state of spiritual crisis. I don't want to suggest that a spiritual crisis must be some sort of emotional handicap, simply that 'crisis' and 'skeptic' share a sense of unsettledness."

A skeptic, and particularly a scientist, does not see "settledness" as a strength, but as a weakness. The strength and success of the scientific method is its honest willingness to change its assertions when confronted by contradictory evidence. Science constantly tests its assertions by seeking out contradictory evidence and by proposing new theories to be tested when such evidence arises.

Contrast that with religion which, as you rightly say, is "settled" about a great many things. When evidence arises that contradicts its "settled" views, religion is astonishingly slow to accept the truth. Look at heliocentrism. The Catholic Church, finally recognized that the earth revolved around the sun in November 1992 (I know you are not Catholic, but I cite them as an example of how a "settled" position is resistant to evidence). Religion and its "settledness" lagged behind scientific skepticism by 377 years. 150 years after Darwin discovered evolution by natural selection, religion's "settledness" still does not accept this scientific fact. One wonders if modern day creationists are out to break the Vatican's 377 year record. Only time will tell.

The thing on which scientists and skeptics are firmly settled is the method of knowing truth. We look at the natural world and put forth explanatory hypotheses that may help us understand it. We then test those hypotheses through rigorously controlled observation, measurement, and analysis. Even when results are analyzed and a conclusion drawn, that conclusion and the data and analysis from which it arises must be published to the scientific community for scrutiny. Only when a conclusion has been studied and replicated by other scientists in the community does it gain hold as an accepted theory. When the theory is confirmed over and over by multiple scientists in multiple disciplines (such as atomic theory, the germ theory of disease, and evolutionary theory), does it become science fact.

Regarding readers of the Bible, you say "there are people who study the Bible in order to prove it wrong because they don't believe in it and are psychologically motivated to justify their unbelief .... There are others who study the Bible in order to prove it right because they believe in it and are spiritually motivated to find justification for their belief."

May I point out the obvious? This is a false dichotomy. There are a great many people, myself included, who treat the claims of the Bible as they would treat claims written in any other book. I have no agenda to prove the Bible false, nor do I have one to prove it true. The Bible is another set of data and any claims it makes about the physical world are scientific claims answerable in principle if not in practice. Take the virgin birth of Jesus. It is highly unlikely that we will get DNA from Jesus to test whether or not he had a father, but such a question is a purely scientific one because it is a claim about the physical world. If by some ridiculously unlikely set of circumstances we did get that DNA, then science could begin to investigate the question.

The morality found in the Bible is also something I come to without an agenda to disprove. When I read that Yahweh commanded people be put to death for gathering sticks on the Sabbath, I do not look for ways to find his actions immoral. I apply my understanding of morality and draw my own conclusions.

You also say, about interpretation of the Bible, "The story of the Bible is not what is commonly thought among believers, and much less among unbelievers. The whole of the larger context is not part of the popular mindset. The fact that people have misunderstood this does not mean that God is false or that the Bible is wrong. It simply verifies the reality of sin and magnifies the grace of God."

Please, please, please understand that you are only one of thousands and thousands of people who will each explain that the rest of the world has interpreted the Bible wrongly. They, like you, will gladly explain that they have figured it out. Whatever your interpretations of Scripture are (other than telling me that they are not what I think they will be, I don't believe you have presented any), you have to agree with me that if God chose the Bible to communicate his message to man, he screwed up royally. In the history of mankind, I don't believe there is a single other text that has failed as miserably as the Bible at clearly communicating an idea to the world.

You then said, "So, you think that I decided that biblical morality is best, whereas others opt for other versions of morality that are equally valid and defensible. This is the ground for moral relativism, which is your skeptical position."

You misunderstand me. I don't think that Biblical morality and humanist morality are "equally valid and defensible." I think much of the morality prescribed by the Bible is crap and not even close to being equal to a morality that strives to increase human well-being and reduce human suffering. Further, I believe that some of the foundations of Biblical morality are even worse than the dictates that spring from them.

The ridiculous idea that faith (believing a proposition in the absence of evidence or even in the presence of contradictory evidence) is a virtue would be laughable if it wasn't so dangerous. The idea that questioning your faith is bad … the idea that infidels are worthy of death … the idea that we are not able to determine what is good … these are all poison pills of religion. I hope I have made it clear that I do not see Biblical morality as "equally valid and defensible."

You then say about the prominence of Christianity, "If you want to argue that human empathy comes from the principles of the survival of the fittest, then why not apply that idea to Christianity itself, since Christianity has proven itself to be the fittest of the religions regarding its survival?"

I am not positively certain of how religion formed in human culture, but I lean toward the growing number of scientists who propose that it is an evolutionary byproduct of another adaptation. A good example of how this may be true is the fact that children are evolved to listen to their parents' instructions unquestioningly. The evolutionary survival value of this is clear. Children who listen to their parents when they say things like "don't swim in that water. There are crocodiles in it" are more likely to survive and pass on their trait for unquestioning obedience than those that don't. Similarly, we have evolved to see agency in things around us whether an agent exists or not.

The meme of religion could be a byproduct of these inherited traits. Remember, evolution applies not just to genes, but to any self-replicating information. That is why meme theory has arisen to explain how certain ideas survive in human culture while others do not. Those ideas that are the best at replicating themselves flourish in human culture. There is a large and growing body of evidence that shows how evolutionary byproducts have contributed to the survival of the religious meme. Consider the Cargo Cults and how quickly their religious meme developed and grew in multiple, geographically diverse cultures.

Phew! Long response to two long posts. I hesitate to add more material, but I would like to ask another question. Does or did God perform miracles? I am not trying to put your round God into a square hole. Feel free to define what a miracle is if you want to claim that he does.

Phillip: Steven, It is not that the church or Christians are slow to change their minds regarding "established facts," but rather it is that all people have difficulty changing the foundations of their "knowledge." And you are also a person, as are scientists. Science today sits in the place that the Catholic Church sat in Galileo's day. It is the scientific worldview that dominates our society, as "a" Christian worldview dominated in Galileo's. And science is also slow to change its mind, so to speak.

You said, "I have no agenda to prove the Bible false, nor do I have one to prove it true." And this is the fly in your ointment. You think that you have an "objective" position from which to judge everything. But you don't. You, like all people, bring various presuppositions to the table with you. There is no such thing as human or scientific objectivity. You need to study more in the philosophy of science.

You said, "The Bible is another set of data and any claims it makes about the physical world are scientific claims answerable in principle if not in practice. Take the virgin birth of Jesus." If you can, note that you are ignoring everything that the Bible says except what it says about the "physical world," even turning everything that it says into something physical. For instance, the birth of Christ is only partly about the birth of Jesus Christ as a human being. And by only considering the physical aspects of Christ, you are guilty of Ebionism,[12] a form of Gnosticism, and the denial of the Trinity. In other words, your view is not Christian, and is opposed to Trinitarian Christianity—not objective by any measure!

Yes, there are a lot of different interpretations of the Bible. That's why it requires the kind of discernment that only regeneration can provide. It cannot be understood correctly apart from the presence and power of the Holy Spirit through regeneration. And rather than being a problem, the variety of interpretations of the regenerate (those of the unregenerate are another matter) provide the texture of diversity to Scripture that helps Christians grow and appreciate other Christians. Christians don't all believe the same things in the same ways, and that provides great lessons in grace, mercy, and forgiveness—sanctification. The joy of life is in the differences. Christianity would be quite boring if everyone believed the same things in the same ways. But the subtlety of this is kept from unbelievers by their unbelief. So, I know that you don't know what I'm talking about. But others do, so I press on.

Here's the proof of what I have said about you: "I think much of the morality prescribed by the Bible is crap .... I believe that some of the foundations of Biblical morality are even worse than the dictates that spring from them." So much for your objectivity. However, if you and I were to sit down and discuss this in detail, I'm pretty sure that I would agree with your assessment

---

12 Ebionism: the beliefs of a Judaistic Christian Gnostic sect of the second century, especially partial observation of Jewish law, rejection of St. Paul and gentile Christianity, acceptance of only one gospel (Matthew), and an early adoptionist Christology.

—IF the Bible teaches what you think it teaches. But it doesn't! That's what you can't see.

"The idea that questioning your faith is bad ... the idea that infidels are worthy of death ..." These are beliefs of the Old Testament and Islam, not Christianity. Yes, Islam finds them in the Old Testament. But Christianity neither believes nor professes either. This is a confusion of many unbelievers. Indeed, Jesus Christ invites questions. He loves them because He knows that God wins all arguments. And He taught that we are to love our enemies, not kill them. Steven, your anger is showing.

You said, "A good example of how this may be true is the fact that children are evolved to listen to their parents' instructions unquestioningly." My God, man! Do you have any children? "Unquestioning obedience" is a behavioral issue not a genetic issue. That means that it is passed on culturally, not genetically. (And this is the role of religion, by the way.)

And now you want to run "miracles" through your meat grinder. You might think that you are scientifically refuting everything that I have said. But you are not. You are only showing your hand, showing your cards (presuppositions) more clearly. Nonetheless, I will concede: the fact of life in Christ is the most important miracle that God has wrought.

See the video: Alexander Tsiaras: *Conception to birth—visualized*, on wwwTED.com.

Steven: Phillip, you said. "It is not that the church or Christians are slow to change their minds regarding 'established facts,' but rather it is that all people have difficulty changing the foundations of their 'knowledge.' And you are also a people, as are scientists. Science today sits in the place that the Catholic Church sat in Galileo's day. It is the scientific worldview that dominates our society, as 'a' Christian worldview dominated in Galileo's. And science is also slow to change its mind, so to speak."

Let's take your assertions in turn. First, you claim that it is not religion that causes people to be settled and intransigent in their beliefs, but rather that everyone has difficulty changing the "foundations of their 'knowledge.'" All I can say is that the evidence does not warrant drawing this conclusion. Religion fights tooth and nail to hang on to dogma in the face of contradictory evidence and we have many examples of this. On the other hand, science works daily to disprove their existing theories and will change them if such evidence arises. Also, how does this jibe with your earlier claim that the non-religious are in spiritual crisis because their beliefs are not "settled" whereas religious folks have beliefs that are "settled"?

You also claim that science today is "in the place that the Catholic Church sat in Galileo's day." This sounds good until you give it a moment's thought. In the U.S. today, a majority of people still cling tightly to beliefs that are in no way scientific (guardian angels, creationism, etc.). Similarly, proven scientific facts are disbelieved and fought by religious apologists such as yourself. Also, there are no dire penalties in place for "science heretics" (if there were such a thing) as there were for anyone who disagreed with Christianity, as Galileo and countless others tragically discovered.

Finally, you mention that science is also slow to change, but scientific reticence is in no way comparable to religion's heel-digging on religious dogma. When completely new theories arise, science doesn't just jump up and say, "Oh. That's it. We were wrong. Ignore the previous body of evidence."

Far more sensibly, science treats new theories with skepticism and requires that evidence be produced for their truth. This evidence must be rigorously confirmed and replicated by the scientific community as a whole before gaining acceptance. This makes perfect sense and has nothing whatsoever in common with the way religious folks cling to dogma. To lay it out, science is always considering new evidence while religion constantly refuses to do so. Finally, in the race to accept new ideas, science beats religion by orders of magnitude. Again, 377 years to accept heliocentricity and 150 years and counting to accept evolution by natural selection.

Next you say with regard to my pointing out of your false dichotomy of scripture readers, "You think that you have an 'objective' position from which to judge everything. But you don't. You, like all people, bring various presuppositions to the table with you. There is no such thing as human or scientific objectivity. You need to study more in the philosophy of science."

Of course no one has a purely objective approach to studying anything, but this is a far cry from your claim that people either come to the Bible with an intent to prove it false or an intent to prove it true. Again, many people like me read the Bible the way we would read any other book. Of course we bring our own intellectual rubric to it. Humans can do nothing else.

That said, the Bible makes very specific claims about the physical world: Jesus didn't have a father. Mary was a virgin when she gave birth. Jesus transformed water into wine. Jesus resurrected a person who had been dead long enough to stink. These are all statements about the physical world.

I freely admit that my bias is that science is the best tool we have to study the physical world and I am more than happy to justify this if you disagree. Do you disagree? Rather than say that I am wrong simply because I have a bias like anyone else, why not point out why I am wrong to think that science is our best tool for understanding such things, if that is what you think. Why wouldn't the transformation of water into wine be studiable by science? Why wouldn't we examine Jesus' DNA if we had it to see if he really didn't have a human father?

You then say in response to my claim that physical claims in the Bible are, in principle, testable by science: "you are ignoring everything that the Bible says except what it says about the 'physical world,' even turning everything that it says into something physical. For instance, the birth of Christ is only partly about the birth of Jesus Christ as a human being. And by only considering the physical aspects of Christ, you are guilty of Ebionism, a form of Gnosticism, and the denial of the Trinity. In other words, your view is not Christian, and is opposed to Trinitarian Christianity—not objective by any measure!"

I commented on both physical and non-physical assertions in the Bible as you should know by reading my post. If these physical claims are important to Christianity, then their truth or falsehood is not irrelevant. The only way we could possibly know their truth is through science, though access to the data is, as I have said, highly unlikely to say the least. If the physical claim of virgin birth, miracles and Christ's resurrection are not important, then you might have a valid criticism. Is that how you feel? It is certainly not how most Christians feel.

By the way, your regular attempts to put me into some sort of box with which you can deal (Ebionism, Gnosticism, etc.) are at best a distraction, and at worst a clumsy attempt at a straw man argument. I don't know if such an approach has worked for you in the past, but it will not work with me. I think I have been very clear about my position and you would do better to address my claims rather than trying to foist the baggage of another world view onto me so that you may dismiss it with arguments practiced for that purpose.

You then backpedal quite a bit on your claim that the vast majority of Christians do not correctly understand Scripture, saying "rather than being a problem, the variety of interpretations of the regenerate (those of the unregenerate are another matter) provide the texture of diversity to Scripture that helps Christians grow and appreciate other Christians."

The "texture of diversity"? Okaaaaay. Phillip, you are forgetting that you presented your minority view of scriptural interpretation to me to refute my criticisms of it. You said my interpretation, like that of most Christians was wrong, not "textured" but wrong. You said in a previous post, "The story of the Bible is not what is commonly thought among believers." Is getting the story wrong part of that texture? Is getting the story wrong something that "helps Christians grow?"

You then say, because I have made value judgments about the morality advocated in Scripture, that I am completely unobjective. You said, "Here's the proof of what I have said about you: 'I think much of the morality prescribed by the Bible is crap .... I believe that some of the foundations of Biblical morality are even worse than the dictates that spring from them.' So much for your objectivity. However, if you and I were to sit down and discuss this in detail, I'm pretty sure that I would agree with your assessment—IF the Bible teaches what you think it teaches. But it doesn't. That's what you can't see."

We have agreed that no one is truly objective, but just because I have read moral lessons in the Bible and found them to be repugnant does not mean that that was what I set out to do. Also, keep in mind that, according to you, I am not alone in my misunderstanding of Scripture. Not only am I not alone, but the "common believer" also misunderstands what the Bible says. I will say it again, if you are right, and if God is using the Bible to get his message out, he has failed miserably, wouldn't you agree?

You then say that Christianity does not squelch the questioning of belief and does not advocate death for the infidel. You say that "These are beliefs of the Old Testament and Islam, not Christianity." This is demonstrably untrue. While Jesus was way ahead of his time with his sermon on the mount, his followers are not always as charitable as he asks them to be, and the violence they perpetrate on out-group infidels is justified by their belief. Throughout the ages, you cannot deny the fact that Christians have killed infidels. While this has tapered off in modern times, it still happens today. With regard to welcoming questions, nothing could be further from the truth. Christianity actually inoculates followers against even considering other views. "Beware of false prophets." Your view of Christianity in these respects is revisionist, and I cannot let you get away with it.

You also claim that the fact that children believe what their parents tell them unquestioningly (interesting scientific studies have been done to prove this) is cultural, not genetic. Interestingly, this phenomenon occurs in every culture in the world no matter how different. It also has reasonable evolutionary grounds. I think you are wrong on this one.

Upon asking you if miracles occur, you say that "the fact of life in Christ is the most important miracle that God has wrought." Very good. Does God do other miracles as well? Let's use a specific example to clarify. Did Christ physically resurrect himself after being dead for 3 days?

Phillip: Steven, you and I are using similar terms but we don't understand them in the same ways, and this makes our communication difficult. You did major in Philosophy, right?

I'm not arguing about religion in general, I'm arguing for Christianity in particular—and for a particular version of Christianity. In the same way that everyone has a particular view of Christianity that is based upon their upbringing, study, faithfulness, etc., so do I. As do you. Our root problem is that you and I use the term "Christianity" to mean different things. It sounds like you have read the Bible and history with Enlightenment categories of disbelief, and kept a record of everything that has gone wrong in Christian history. Granted, that's a lot. Christianity cannot be understood by seeing it through the lives and ideas of Christians alone. Doing that will give you an understanding of Churchianity, but not Christianity.

Nonetheless, Christians can and do learn much from the historical, theological, and philosophical errors made by other Christians. Learning from the errors of the past provides very important information and lessons. It seems that you look at the historical data and throw out the proverbial baby with the bathwater. While Christians work hard to preserve the baby. And you are right that a lot of Christians mistakenly preserve a lot of the bathwater. This is where discernment comes in.

The fact that science enjoys much of the moral perspective that it inherited from Christianity does not means that science is not the dominant worldview today, as Churchianity was in yesteryears.

All change happens faster today than it did in the past. It's a function of population. So, arguments that ancient Churchianity changed slower than modern science is moot.

Regarding the objectivity issue: Good, you see that you are prejudiced, as am I. You said that "Jesus didn't have a father," but He did—and this is no minor issue, but is at the very crux of our disagreement. This is a perfect illustration of what you don't see because you look through the glasses of materialism. Because you are looking for Jesus' DNA to establish His virgin birth, you are unable to begin to commence to discover the meaning and necessity of the immaculate conception or any other of the biblical miracles.

You are like a little boy who was told of a great treasure. When the little boy grew up he became a treasure hunter. And one day he found and ancient, gold plated, diamond studded treasure box buried on an obscure island. Excitedly he brought the box aboard his treasure ship. But when he opened the treasure box it was empty, and in a fit of anger threw it overboard. (None of this story is true. Yet, it illustrates a greater truth—if not about you specifically, then about human nature generally.)

The stories in the Bible are true, especially the story of Balaam's talking ass (Numbers 22-24).[13]

You said, "The only way we could possibly know their truth is through science, though access to the data is, as I have said, highly unlikely to say the least." Again, note your language: you say here that the only truth you will accept is scientific truth, by which you mean materialism. Then you demand materialistic proof for non-materialism matters. It is an absurd request.

Lastly, it is true that my charges of Ebionism and Gnosticism don't really fit. You are more likely an Epicurean.[14]

---

13 See Ross, Phillip A. *Peter's Vision of the End in Second Peter*, Pilgrim Platform, Marietta, Ohio, 2010, "Balaam," p. 98-102.
14 In popular parlance, Epicureanism is the devotion to pleasure, comfort, and

On the textured diversity of biblical truth: Yes, I said your assessment is wrong. Thus, it is outside of the textured diversity of biblical truth. The fact that believers can get the biblical story wrong and still be saved is most surely an indication of the breadth of God's mercy. But there is a limit to His mercy, and I pray that you not discover it. Rather than having failed miserably with regard to the Bible, God has in fact succeeded to use the Bible exactly as He set out to do.

Christianity is almost twice as successful in terms of raw numbers as it's nearest competitor (Islam). And, interestingly, it tends to keep the worst of the pagans and heretics out, which protects those in the fold. And as for not allowing questions: some denominations are better than others regarding this. The Catholics are the worst because they have the most intricate system that they have to maintain—and that's where you began. That view of Christianity in in your DNA, so to speak. In addition, you may have felt the knobby end of the stick in this regard because some people who ask questions have no desire to find answers. They just want to prove some point or another, many teaching nuns are quick to put such a spirit to flight.

My view of Christianity is not revisionist, but is correctionist. I find that the Bible teaches the progressive revelation of Jesus Christ in history, which means that true Christianity is not ancient Christianity, but future Christianity—the future that God decreed from the beginning.[15] God is growing Christianity in the same way that He is growing Christians. Maturity takes time, but unfortunately time alone does not produce maturity. The errors and idiocies of childhood do not permanently mar the man.

Oh, and Christ did not resurrect Himself. God the Father did that. You should know that.

---

high living, with a certain nicety of style.
15 Again, Ross, Phillip A. *Peter's Vision of Christ's Purpose in First Peter* (2011) and *Peter's Vision of The End in Second Peter* (2011), Pilgrim Platform, Marietta, Ohio.

Steven: Phillip, it seems that we may be reaching some agreement after all this time. You said, "I'm not arguing about religion in general, I'm arguing for Christianity in particular—and for a particular version of Christianity." You also said, "Christians can and do learn much from the historical, theological, and philosophical errors made by other Christians."

Let's find some common ground by setting aside your view of Christianity for a moment and focusing on those worldviews that you and I both seem to agree are wrong. Islam, Judaism, Buddhism, Hellenistic polytheism, belief in Norse Gods, belief in Babylonian deities, and much of Christianity, if I understand you correctly, are all incorrect at best and viciously divisive, violent worldviews at worst. They have driven humanity to some of the most awful atrocities imaginable (remember, I am not talking about your particular religious views).

So, can we agree that these other faiths are wrong, their followers deluded, and that they should be discouraged. If so, we can leave them out of our conversation going forward. I wish to make no more statements that conflate your worldview with theirs. Rather, I want to focus exclusively on what you believe. What do you think?

Phillip: That's what I'm focusing on, but please don't think that it is my view exclusively. There are actually a lot of people who share various aspects of it. And I also find Epicureanism to be in error, as well. You?

Steven: Excellent! Now that that is out of the way, tell me what proper Christianity is.

Phillip: Steven, I'm afraid that I may have given you the wrong impression here. This ground is not likely to be as common as I previously hoped, but we'll see. While we can leave discussion of other religions out of our conversation, I do not believe that all religion is "viciously divisive, violent ... driven humanity to some of the most awful atrocities imaginable."

You seem to group all religions into a single category, which is an over simplification of the reality. So, let me begin by roughly sketching a better analysis of religious history. The analysis is in story form, not philosophical or theological assertions, because human reality exists in time and is subject to the vicissitudes of time. We do not live in a timeless realm of logical, idealistic perfection.

Yahweh Elohim (the Trinitarian God) created humanity in His/ Their image. We don't need to go back any further than this for our current purposes. So, the first expression of God in human history was Trinitarian. Christ was with God and the Holy Spirit from before time began. There is/was no reason to doubt God's veracity, so it is axiomatically assumed at this point in order to understand both God and ourselves. However, this expression was given at the infancy of humanity, and the expression matched the ability of humanity to understand it. It was given in covenantal seed form regarding the two trees in the Garden, and it was given negatively in order to provide the maximum human freedom possible. Don't eat of the one tree because the consequence will lead to human extinction, but eat of the other because it provides for eternal human sustainability.

The Serpent, who used to be the highest of God's ambassadors but who had disagreed with God in the past, then intervened by suggesting that God was not who He said He was, and therefore he argued that what God had said about the two trees was not accurate. The point here is the introduction of sin, which involves an opinion other than God's regarding God's prohibitions. Sin is defined as doubting God's Word (His story). Human beings must of logical necessity assume some beginning point. Logic does not exist without context. Even the Serpent began with God's assertions, against which he raised doubt.

The details of the story are more complex than stated here, but for our purposes we will omit them in order to show where I'm going with this line of thought.

There is one true God manifest in three divine Persons—Father, Son, and Holy Spirit. Doubting God led to two misunderstandings or misinterpretations regarding God: 1) that God is monotheistic and 2) that God is polytheistic. Both of these errors manifested very early in human history—at the point of doubting God's assessment of things, doubting that God is who He says He is. Both of these positions are theistic, and doubt taken to its extreme then led to the ultimate doubt, which is doubting theism altogether. The struggles that issued from these various doubts are documented in the Old Testament and the New Testament.

Thus, there is one true God who is Trinitarian. And lots of false god positions: i.e., monotheism, polytheism, and atheism. All of the theistic expressions are corruptions of the real Trinitarian God in that they do not include the fullness of God's actual character. Some focus on monotheism (Judaism, elements of Hinduism and Islam), some focus on polytheism (paganism, animism, elements of Hinduism), some focus on atheism (Epicureanism, Buddhism, elements of Hinduism, Confucianism, humanism and its variants).

In addition, some believers of these various positions actually believe in the Trinitarian God, but don't realize it. However, when presented with the facts, they convert their beliefs to Trinitarianism. While others are virulently opposed to God choose to believe anything, except Trinitarianism. When confronted with the facts, they hold fast to their various positions in denial of Trinitarianism. Again, the reality is much more complex than this.

Nonetheless, there are some people in each group who will concur with God's Truth and others who will not. Even among Trinitarians, there are people like Balaam and other false prophets, who replicate the ideas of Trinitarianism ("having the appearance of godliness, but denying its power" (2 Tim. 3:5), but who attempt to use it for their own purposes. We call them religious shysters today.

Biblical Trinitarianism (Christianity) is therefore the first and only true expression of God. There have always been believers and unbelievers in the world. In the Old Testament believers follow the lineage of Seth and unbelievers follow the lineage of Cain.

This description is very brief. To understand it, much reading is required.

Steven: Phillip, thank you for this. Let me restate as best I can, though briefly as I am on a brief break from work. The existence of the trinitarian God is assumed as an axiom in your worldview. There are various other religious viewpoints who assume other versions of this axiom, but they are mistaken, though they may come to realize this mistake when they are shown certain facts. The story of creation as told in Genesis is literally true and recounts for us the act of original sin which was Eve's disobedience of God.

How did I do?

Phillip: Not bad. A few areas will probably land us in disagreement. The Trinitarian God is more than an axiom, but is initially assumed in order to understand the context of the biblical stories. God's reality is manifest everywhere, but unbelievers do not accept the data as originating in God. The fullest expression of the Trinitarian God is Jesus Christ. other positions do not comprehend the whole of the Trinitarian God, and are therefore corruptions of His truth and wholeness.

Not all unbelievers who are shown various facts are able to understand them correctly because they deny the truth and wholeness of the Trinitarian God. Their axiomatic assumption of God is limited, conditional, or corrupt in that some other assumption supersedes it. The correct axiomatic assumption regarding the Trinitarian God is that God always precedes and supersedes everything.

The stories of the Bible are literature and must be read as literature. Thus, they are literarily (not literally) true. They are all true, but as the story I provided a couple of posts earlier about the treasure box, the "facts" of their truth are not always scientifically measurable. Some truth is analogical, some is didactic, some is poetic, some is parabolic, some is narrative, some is historic, etc.

When I tell you a story about myself that illustrates something true about my character, the truth regarding my character is not dependent upon the historical veracity of the story. For instance, I could retell a fictional story in order to illustrate the true characteristic—and there would be nothing false, untrue, or untoward about the use of the story as an illustration regarding some actual characteristic of me. So, it would be absurd for someone to say that, because the story is fictional, there must therefore be some deceit or falsehood regarding the character trait that it illustrates. Also, when the story is personal and anecdotal it adds to the truth being illustrated.

Steven: So, God is not just an axiom. Rather, we assume his existence so that we can understand what is written in the Bible. Evidence of God's existence is everywhere, but only people who already believe in God can recognize it. The trinitarian God is the most complete understanding of God and other religions are not totally wrong, but do not understand all of what is God. Not all unbelievers who are presented with the specific facts that are evidence of the truth of the Trinitarian God will understand them correctly, because one must already believe in the existence of the Trinitarian God in order to understand this evidence. The correct assumption is that the Trinitarian God exists and that this assumption supersedes any other knowledge you may acquire.

The Bible is written in several literary forms, and so while it always communicates truth, the stories in it did not always literally happen.

Am I getting it?

By the way, I completely understand and respect your literary approach to Scripture. I must ask a specific question, though. Do you believe the Adam, Eve, serpent original sin story is literally true? That it actually happened as described?

Phillip: Steven, On the one hand you are able to do the reflective listening and reproduce what I have said. But on the other hand you then ask if the Adam, Eve, serpent original sin story actually happened as described. And by asking such a question, you reveal that you don't understand what I'm talking about. You insist on steam rolling over the texture that I have set out in order to flatten it out so that you can (probably) point out that you have never heard a talking snake. Which in your mind would then destroy the veracity of the story.

Nonetheless, did the story actually happen as it is recorded in Scripture? That information is not available. All we have is the story. The purpose of the story is to communicate. And the purpose of communication is to share information. So, does the story communicate? Yes. Does it share information? Yes. Is the information valid and useful? Yes.

So, how would you reply if I answered "Yes, it is literally true."?

And how would you reply if I answered "No, it isn't."?

Steven: Phillip, I asked if the Adam and Eve story actually happened because I want to understand what you believe. Your statement of what you believe should be honest and true and have nothing to do with what you think I will say about it. During our long discussion, you have regularly accused me of misunderstanding your position, and I have no doubt that you are right in those accusations. I want to go down a different road at this point. I want to hear from you what your position is and I will not criticize it as you tell me what it is. I want to understand.

As for the literal truth of the Adam and Eve story, I think you did a wonderful job of pointing out that Scripture, like other literature, has portions that are to be interpreted as poetic and others that are rightly interpreted as being records of actual events that really happened. All I am asking is how you interpret the story of Adam and Eve that you related. It sounds as though you are agnostic on the subject when you say, "Nonetheless, did the story actually happen as it is recorded in Scripture? That information is not available." and that is a good enough answer for me.

Did I get the rest of my summary correct?

Phillip: Steven, Yes, your reflective listening skills are doing fine. And I appreciate that you want to understand what I believe.

If you really want to understand what I believe, then you should read my books. I suggest that because I write with the hope of undoing false understanding and false expectations so that more realistic understandings and expectations can be found. The central problem that people have, in my opinion, is undoing the crap that has been accepted as truth in their past.

For instance, you grew up Catholic—my condolences. Catholics have a lot of baggage to unload before they can accept truth, in my opinion. But that doesn't mean that everything that the Roman Catholic Church believes or has done is wrong. For the most part, their beliefs and practices are inadequate to the current reality. They are stuck in old patterns of thinking, as well as in wrong patterns. Sorting it all out is a huge task.

As for Adam and Eve in Genesis, I believe that what the Bible communicates to us about God, Satan, ourselves and sin is absolutely true. The method of conveying that truth is narrative or story. And in order to understand what is being communicated, the reader must "buy the premise." Are you a Star Trek fan? If so, in order to appreciate Star Trek, viewers must buy the premise of space travel and alien life forms, etc. If you don't do that, you will miss the deeper meanings of the various stories. Same with the Bible.

Does that mean that serpents talk? Steven, have you never seen a serpent talk? Just watch INSP (the Inspiration channel of cable TV) and you will see them on a regular basis. Is this what the Bible means by using a talking serpent? Absolutely. So, it's true. The literary device for this is called personification, treating the snake as if it is a person. But also treating the person as if he is a snake. Yes, yes, yes! This is absolutely true!

The better question to ask about the story is not whether it is true or not, but what does it mean? Accept the premise, and then extract the meaning. Then ask if the meaning is true, valid, useful, etc.

Steven: Phillip, I am glad to hear that I am getting it right so far. I will continue.

Much of your worldview is a departure from the traditional Christian theological worldviews of the past which were incorrect. Catholicism and the early Christian Church got it wrong. They adopted beliefs and practices that were inadequate for the proper understanding of the triune God. Their patterns of thinking are old and wrong and it is quite a difficult exercise to sort out the real truth. It is not until very recently that anyone really understood Christianity.

The message of Adam and Eve is true whether or not the actual physical events are true. The truth of the actual events does not matter, rather one must read the story in the context of what might be fictional events to get to the true meaning of the story which is what is crucial. Correct?

So, what is the true meaning of the Adam and Eve story?

Phillip: Steven, No, no. My beliefs are not a departure from traditional Christian Protestant Reformed theological beliefs. To say that Catholicism and the early Christian Church got it wrong says far too much. Many things were right according to what was known at the time, but inadequate for us today, other things were wrong. Belief in the Trinity has always existed, even in the Old Testament. It is not true that only until recently have people properly understood Christianity. Your effort to boil it all down into some simplistic form is ill advised. Doing this involves the steam roller or the forcing round things into square holes, as previously discussed.

Think of Christianity as a tree. It began as an acorn, then became a sprout, then a plant, then a small tree, a medium tree, an old tree, etc. At every point it was both different and yet always the same tree. The tree is viewed at different times by different people from different perspectives, but the tree is always a true tree.

The message conveyed by the Adam and Eve story about God, Satan, human beings and sin is true when correctly understood. There actually were true historic events at the dawn of humanity that correspond to the stories of Adam and Eve, but the exact character of that correspondence is not available to us today. All we have today are the stories and the messages.

The true meaning of the Adam and Eve story depends a great deal upon the purpose for which said meaning will be employed. I'm not saying that it isn't true, I'm saying that the truth of the message about God, Satan, human beings, and sin needd to be adapted to the audience and the purpose for which this information is being presented because truth that does not connect with real people may as well be false because the message is not correctly transmitted. For truth to be true, it must be communicated, correctly sent and correctly recieved. Otherwise we are just singing in the shower (to ourselves). True communication requires both transmission and reception. If either break down, the communication fails and the message cannot be evaluated as being true or false.

So, in our case the very first true meaning of the Adam and Eve story is that you, Steven, are a guilty sinner.

Steven: Wow! The Bible references me specifically! I'm somebody!

So, your beliefs do not depart from traditional Christian Protestant Reformed theological beliefs and are for all practical purposes the same. The early Christian Church didn't "get it wrong" as much as they held some beliefs that were right given the knowledge they had at the time, but that would not be right today. Other things they believed/practiced were simply wrong. The idea of a trinitarian God has existed since the beginning of time and is expressed in the text of the Old Testament. People have indeed properly understood Christianity even with ideas that predate yours. It is not proper to compare and contrast belief systems as a whole since doing so is reductionist and results in incorrect conclusions.

The nature of Christianity can be compared to a tree. It starts from a single idea and grows into different expressions, but is always the same thing. Different people view the tree from different perspectives, and though they may think they are seeing different things, they are all seeing the same thing.

The message of the Biblical creation myth is true (that human beings sin against God). There were actual historical events at the dawn of humanity that correspond to the story, but we have no way of knowing how closely the events in the story correspond to actual events.

The truth of the Adam and Eve story does not exist independently from human perception of it. It needs to be adapted to each audience that hears it otherwise the message will not be communicated and it will do no more good than a false message.

The true message of Adam and Eve is that each of us individually disobeys God.

So, a few question come up. I intend them to help me further understand your view, not as attacks. You will see that each one asks for more information.

First, you relate that "some" of the early church beliefs were correct given the knowledge they had at the time and that "some" were just plain wrong. I think some examples of beliefs in each category would help me understand this better.

Second, you state that the Adam and Eve story does correspond to actual historical events, but that we have no access to knowledge about those events and so cannot know how close the correspondence is. What do you think is the range of possible correspondence? Could it be literally true? Could it be that the only correspondence is that people came along who disobeyed God?

Phillip: Steven, I think that you may be used to contemplating specific doctrines philosophically, and finding various philosophical and scientific things wrong with them. But I'm not providing doctrines. Rather, I hope to provide a perspective from which the Bible can be productively read and understood.

Rather than thinking about traditional Christian Protestant Reformed doctrine as a fixed thing, think of it as a trajectory of correct biblical understanding. My beliefs fall along that trajectory. So, some people who don't take the whole trajectory into consideration may find my beliefs to be "the same" as theirs, but others may find them to "depart," in that they are farther along the trajectory than theirs are.

Reductionism is a problem. You might want to read the book, *The Reduction of Christianity: Dave Hunt's Theology of Cultural Surrender*, by Gary DeMar, Dominion Press, 1988.

It's not that the tree analogy of Christianity "grows into different expressions," but that it simply grows—but growing doesn't make it something else. Some of the "different expressions" are true and faithful, and some aren't. But the point of the analogy is that Christianity itself grows and matures, as individual Christians also do. People can go astray at any point along the growth trajectory by overemphasis or underemphasis of various ideas. Nonetheless, there is a trajectory that conforms to the tradition and faithfulness of the past while at the same time growing beyond traditional formulations without destroying them. When

I grew into a man, my childhood was not destroyed, nor was it "wrong," though I don't understand things like I did then. Error helps to refine the truth.

The essence of Christianity is wholeness. But saying that, I must warn you that the idea of wholeness has been used by a lot of non-Christians, people who try to integrate all of the world's religions into a whole. But that is not what Christianity does. Christianity believes the First Commandment against false gods. There is only one true God, who is Trinitarian, and a lot of false gods which are actually unreal. So, summing up all religions into a religious soup doesn't add up the Trinitarian God. Nonetheless, God provides wholeness in this world. What makes up a "whole?"

You and I are whole individuals, but does our wholeness include our families, the food we eat, air we breathe, or our children, etc.? These things are "outside" of our bodies, yet they are involved in our wholeness. People without arms are still whole people, right? Even though "part" of them is missing. What is wholeness? Ultimately, God provides the wholeness of the world, and as with us, the wholeness of the world includes more than the planet earth. The sun and the moon are also involved in the wholeness of the earth.

May I suggest that wholeness is related to purpose. It is the purpose of a thing that determines the sort of wholeness we attribute to it. Does the world have a purpose? God says it does—to serve His glory. But you will also say that the world has a purpose, right?

And here is where evolution fails. Random chaos is antithetical to purpose. Surely you are familiar with teleology.

Your request for examples of "right" and "wrong" traditional doctrines is a pretty large request. To get a real understanding of this will require reading at least a shelf of books because it is not sufficient to just say this or that is right or wrong without delving into the specifics of why and how and in what sense. Nonetheless, the Reformed doctrine of predestination may provide an example.

Augustine and Calvin are credited with this doctrine, though it is in Scripture (Isaiah 46:10, etc.) and in the statement from the Council of Orange, 529 A.D. But Calvin understood it differently than Augustine, partly because of the advances in science and theology. And, of course, those who believe it today have different understandings of than did either Calvin or Augustine. Now to answer the question of exactly how it is different today involves a lot. But you know a lot about science, so try to figure something out. How might such a doctrine be possible today?

Adam and Eve: First, to say that the biblical story does in fact correlate to some specific history, without knowing the specifics of the correlation, is an act of faith not science. In a sense, it's like the chicken and the egg problem.

The Bible says that God created Adam (אדם). What exactly does it say? "Then God said, 'Let us make man in our image, after our likeness'" (Genesis 1:26). The issue here is that "man" is a "kind" or species. Today we know only of man as a group or set (think mathematical Set Theory), composed of individuals. But no single individual could ever exist alone for very long. Yet, God said that He created one man, and then from that one He wrought another, and from them came humanity. Logically, there must have been a first "prototype." Yet, no individual prototype could ever exist alone. It could not interbreed with apes or whatever, just as we can't today.

The theory of evolution tries to explain this naturally, without God, by adding the magic sauce of time. The idea suggests that, given enough time, anything is possible. So, random errors of genetic code transmission eventually produced something infinitely better. Yea, right! Improvement through error.

When you ask if the story is "literally true," what are you asking for? Driver's licensees for Adam and Eve? The Bible essentially says that it is a mystery that God accomplished. Somehow humanity got started, and we can't go back and understand how it happened. All we have are the old stories. So, the better question is what can we learn about God and ourselves from the story? Is it useful or helpful? It is. God made us good, but something happened and we lost our goodness. Does this ring true today? Sure it does. God wants to fix the problem. Do we want it fixed? Ultimately, it comes down to the individual, do you want to be fixed? Or are you happy in your brokenness? You might tell me that you personally are not broken, but can you make that argument for humanity? And if humanity is broken, then are you an instance of broken humanity? Etc.

Steven: Phillip, you said that you are not communicating a doctrine, but rather a way of seeing things which will help people better understand what is written in the Bible.

Rather than thinking of traditional doctrinal statements as static, you suggest that I think of them as paths along which correct understanding of the Bible develops over time. Your own beliefs are not fixed, but are only a single point on the continuing path of development. Your current beliefs will be inadequate for future times just as older beliefs are inadequate today. Beliefs that are at different points on the trajectory are not the same nor are they different. Such judgments cannot be made about the beliefs themselves, but only their relative positions on the development path.

I have misunderstood the tree analogy you used to explain Christianity. Growth entails change, but does not mean that the thing growing changes from one thing to another. The key is that the growth is along a specific path, and some beliefs will stray from this path perhaps by overemphasizing or minimizing certain aspects of their beliefs. The fact that beliefs change over time along this trajectory does not mean that Christianity changes. Rather, the Christian moves on to more mature beliefs without destroying the beliefs from which they have moved. It is similar to when a child grows into an adult.

The essence of Christianity is God's wholeness in that boundaries between objects in reality are impossible to clearly define. We cannot define distinct entities in the absence of the things which give them context, like our bodies and the surrounding environment. This results in an infinite progress away from individual distinctions toward the whole which is the Trinitarian God.

One possible way to make quasi-distinctions is through purpose. For each thing being identified, one can ask what is its purpose. This is where evolution fails as it completely ignores the idea of purpose because it is random chaos. Evolution cannot explain the order in our natural world.

To provide examples of past doctrines that are "right" (follow the correct trajectory of ideas over time) and that are "wrong" (stray from the correct trajectory of ideas over time) is a substantial request. A true understanding of any example would require significant amounts of research and study. That said, the doctrine of Predestination may present a reasonable example.

Calvin and Augustine both believed in predestination, though each understood it differently. Calvin was able to understand it through advances in science and technology, while Augustine was not. Science today might understand it differently, perhaps the determinism of mechanistic materialism.

The assertion that the Biblical story of Adam and Eve correlates to some historic events is made in the absence of evidence. There is neither inductive nor deductive reason to believe this. It is a matter of faith. In a sense it is like the chicken and egg problem. [I can't help an editorial comment, though not a combative one. I simply want to point out that evolution says that the egg came first.]

You interpret the creation story as showing that God created man as a distinct species and that He purposefully created more than one because such is necessary for mankind to survive. The theory of evolution tries to explain this by saying that given enough time "anything is possible" and random changes in genetic code produced better, more complex organisms. This is like saying that a lot of random errors can, over time, produce elegant complexity. Such an idea is ludicrous [I agree, by the way.]

The factual truth of aspects of a literal interpretation of the Adam and Eve story cannot be known. Somehow we got started and the details are unknowable. It is better to ask what we can learn from this story that we accept through faith. We can know that God made the first people good people. Something happened and people lost their goodness. This resonates today. We are all broken and God offers to fix us. Perhaps I don't feel I am broken, but humanity as a whole certainly is. If it is, how can any individual claim not to be?

Am I still getting it right? Is this a productive exercise? Have we progressed enough for you to feel confident that I have an understanding of your beliefs? Should we go further?

Phillip: Sure, your listening skills are fine. (What did the advanced evolutionary chicken egg come from, since there is only scientific evidence that chickens lay chicken eggs?) I'm not sure that you have an adequate understanding of what I'm saying, but you have summed it up well. So, take us further.

Steven: Well, Phillip, the vast gulf between my world view and yours is our difference regarding evidentialism. You begin your worldview by positing the existence of a Trinitarian God as a matter of faith. I begin mine by positing the value of evidence and induction as a means of learning true things about our universe. My axioms have evidence to support their truth value. I have not seen any such evidence for yours.

I do not think this is a chasm that either of us is willing to cross in either direction. If I point out to you that some of your beliefs are inconsistent with evidence, this will not sway you because faith supersedes evidence for you. And so we have constructed a long thread of back and forth postings, me claiming that your beliefs are not justified and you claiming that evidence is inferior to faith.

Phillip: Steven, your analysis agrees with mine. Our differences pertain to philosophical method. You are an evidentialist and I am an presuppositionalist. Or in more traditional language, you are an unbeliever and I am a believer. Theologically, this division was explored in the Clark-Van Til Controversy.[16] Whatever else it is, it is not something that will be decided in this discussion.

My critique of evidentialism is that it begins with evidence, while the nub of the issue pertains to the fact that there is any evidence to consider. Thus, evidentialism is guilty of ignoring its own presuppositions. It is circular in that it begins with evidence in order to prove evidence. Whereas presuppotionalism begins with God in order to establish and define the evidence. Both positions begin by assuming things. I assume God, and you assume not-God.

You will argue against this by saying that your position assumes neither God nor not-God, and is "objective." However, the issue is about what constitutes "objectivity." I say that objectivity is not possible apart from God because God created everything, and to separate things from their Creator is to remove an important element of their context. And you will say that I am obscuring objectivity by imposing God upon it. And I will argue that I am not imposing God upon it, but that God has imposed Himself upon it, and I am simply recognizing that reality, which your are denying and ignoring.

You argue from a materialist position, but if you consider that all known material is composed of smaller and smaller units that are more accurately described as energy, then your position could also be described as energist (everything is made of energy, as opposed to a *materialist*). The parallels between energy and

---

16 Hoeksema. Herman. *The Clark-Van Til Controversy*, The Trinity Foundation, 2005.

spirit are many, but the Christian would continue to posit that God (or the wholeness of human energy wherein the whole is greater than the sum of the parts because it includes a different order, realm or dimension) is personal.

I cannot make you see/understand my position, though I see yours. I see your position because it is the natural (Adamic) position into which all people are born. My position can only be seen/understood by those who are regenerate. So, while you are able to lip-sync my position through reflective listening, your words are empty of the reality, "having the appearance of godliness, but denying its power" (2 Timothy 3:5).

I do not claim that "evidence is inferior to faith," but that faith in the Trinitarian God of the Bible provides the best, most consistent and realistic ground upon which evidence can exist for consideration. And furthermore, I contend that evidence without the proper context is deceptive. For instance, just because one of my hairs is conclusively established to be at the crime scene, does not mean that I'm guilty. Time plays a key role in that my hair may have been deposited at the crime scene long before the crime took place and in some other context. Time is always the magic sauce of evolutionists. It plays the role that "God" played in previous times by "explaining" how things came to be as they are.

Steven: Time is not the "magic sauce" of evolution which cannot accurately be said to have a "magic" anything. You do not understand natural selection and the proof of geologic timescales. Evolution is not, as you say "random" and does not assert that "anything is possible."

By the way, how do you reconcile your criticism of evidence and science with the fact that almost every convenience you enjoy (including the computer on which you are typing) was brought to you by induction and evidence?

Phillip: The following is a summary of the modern synthesis —from: Wikipedia/ Modern_evolutionary_synthesis.

The modern synthesis bridged the gap between experimental geneticists and naturalists, and between palaeontologists. It states that:

1. All evolutionary phenomena can be explained in a way consistent with known genetic mechanisms and the observational evidence of naturalists.

2. Evolution is gradual: small genetic changes, recombination ordered by natural selection. Discontinuities amongst species (or other taxa) are explained as originating gradually through geographical separation and extinction (not saltation).

3. Natural selection is by far the main mechanism of change; even slight advantages are important when continued. The object of selection is the phenotype in its surrounding environment.

4. The role of genetic drift is equivocal. Though strongly supported initially by Dobzhansky, it was downgraded later as results from ecological genetics were obtained.

5. Thinking in terms of populations, rather than individuals, is primary: the genetic diversity existing in natural populations is a key factor in evolution. The strength of natural selection in the wild is greater than previously expected; the effect of ecological factors such as niche occupation and the significance of barriers to gene flow are all important.

6. In palaeontology, the ability to explain historical observations by extrapolation from microevolution to macroevolution is proposed. Historical contingency means explanations at different levels may exist. Gradualism does not mean constant rate of change.

My comments:
1. As previously discussed, no one argues against microevolution. And no one has observational evidence for macroevolution.

What we see is limited variation within species, but not one species becoming another species.

2. *Gradual* means time, and is the magic sauce.

3. "Natural selection is the nonrandom process by which biologic traits become either more or less common in a population as a function of differential reproduction of their bearers." A nonrandom process is an orderly process. Again, natural selection pertains to microevolution because one species cannot breed with another by definition. Besides, even if it means macroevolution, where did the order come from?

4. *Equivocal* means "Open to two or more interpretations; or of uncertain nature or significance; or (often) intended to mislead; open to question; uncertain."

5. Again, 5 applies to microevolution.

6. Explains macroevolution by extrapolation from microevolution. Whatever extrapolation is it means that there is no direct observable evidence. It's a guess—right or wrong, good or bad—but a speculation.

I have no problems with science and technology, which developed out of the worldview of Western Christianity.

Steven: I understand that the Christian church funded scientists in the middle ages. But that is not what you are claiming. You are claiming that science (rigorous inductive reasoning that is evidentiary in nature) came from the faith-based Christian worldview. Can you detail how the one idea lead to the other?

Steven: By the way, if you believe in "microevolution," then you believe in evolution.

Phillip: Notice your own words: that we are talking about *belief* in evolution. Microevolution is simply variations within species, and the science behind this is solid. Macroevolution involves the theory of one species mutating into another. And while there are many similarities between species that give rise to such speculation, the similarities can also be explained by reference to a common creator and a common world of existence.

Also notice that you haven't addressed my comments on evolution.

Steven: I used "belief" because that's the word you used. Will you please notice that my usual retort is the correct one. You do not understand evolution. If you did, you would not make the same mistakes about it over and over.

We've been over this already. The information you provided (rather than explaining in your own words) establishes that Christians did science. That is true. They did. But that is not what you claim. You claim that an evidential epistemology where rigorously governed induction is the only source of truth … came from Christian theology. Explain or stop making the silly claim.

As to your comments on evolution, they are listed below with my responses.

1. As previously discussed, no one argues against microevolution. And no one has observational evidence for macroevolution. What we see is limited variation within species, but not one species becoming another species.

There are a great many things that we know through observing data that we did not see directly. We have never observed dinosaurs living and breathing, but we know that they did. We have never observed Jesus walking and talking, but historical evidence shows that he did. We do not know these things through faith, but through evidence. YOU DON'T HAVE TO DIRECTLY OBSERVE A PAST PHENOMENON TO SEE EVIDENCE THAT IT HAPPENED/IS TRUE!!! The evidence in fossils, genetics and geographic distribution of life is clear evidence that species gradually change into other species. The changes are MICRO and cumulative. For pity's sake, READ A BOOK ON EVOLUTION! There is more evidence that species have a common ancestor than there is that atoms make up matter and that germs cause disease.

2. Gradual means time, and is the magic sauce.

Gradual does mean time, but time is not a "magic sauce." Time is time. The evidence for an earth that is billions, not thousands, of years old is overwhelming, not that evidence matters much to you, so I'm not sure why we're having this conversation.

3. "Natural selection is the nonrandom process by which biologic traits become either more or less common in a population as a function of differential reproduction of their bearers. A nonrandom process is an orderly process. Again, natural selection pertains to microevolution because one species cannot breed with another by definition. Besides, even if it means macroevolution, where did the order come from?"

The order comes from natural selection. Some number of mutations /variations occur within a species over generations. A variation that helps the organism to survive and pass on its genes (including the genes for the variation) is *naturally selected* to thrive. Variations that do not help the organism to pass on its genes (including the variation) are *naturally selected* not to thrive. So, the genes that survive and are passed on are not random. They are the *opposite of random*. They are "selected" for survival by nature, and no intelligent agent is necessary.

4. Equivocal means "Open to two or more interpretations; or of uncertain nature or significance; or (often) intended to mislead; open to question; uncertain."

Genetic drift is another possible explanation for some of the variations that occur in species. It is not "intended to mislead," though I think its fair to say that your use of that definition is.

5. Again, 5 applies to microevolution.

Microevolution is the only kind of evolution there is. You do not understand it. Try this thought experiment. You are standing in front of an impossibly long line of rabbits. Each rabbit in the line is the ancestor of the one in front of it. As you walk down the line, eventually you will see subtle changes in the rabbit, though no two adjoining animals in the line will look very different from each other. As you progress, the animals in the line will become less "rabbity" until, if you walk long enough, the animals won't look like rabbits at all. At some point, let's say you are far enough back to be able to make a hairpin turn down another line that leads to modern day leopards. As you walk down this line, again, no two adjoining animals will look very different, but as you continue down the many, many, many generations, the animals will begin to look more "leopardy," until you end up at the present day leopard. At no specific point in the line will you be able to say of two adjoining animals, "This is a leopard and this is not." It is all done through many generations of the microevolution you have already said you understand.

6. Explains macroevolution by extrapolation from microevolution. Whatever extrapolation is it means that there is no direct observable evidence. It's a guess—right or wrong, good or bad—but a speculation.

Many, many evidence-based conclusions are about things that happened in the past that we did not directly observe. Every scientific study of a crime scene, every measurement and theory of cosmology, every time you visit a doctor who examines an injury, in all of these cases and many, many more, evidence helps us decide the truth of things that happened in the past that we did not directly observe. Speciation in evolution (what you misleadingly call "macro" evolution is backed up by 150 years worth of collected evidence in multiple disciplines, by multiple scientists. Your demand that science only deal with present phenomenon demonstrates that you do not understand science.

Phillip: Steven, you used "belief" because there is no other way to say what your relationship to evolution is.

If you have an interest in understanding the relationship between Christianity and science, you can read a book or two. Your desire for me to boil it down so you can shoot it down will only satisfy your lust for straw men to slay. I have given you sufficient information for serious inquiry.

Regarding evolution, you and I are talking about different things or aspects of the idea, which is why we talk past one another. You are talking about microevolution and the evidence thereof, which I am not disputing. I understand the argument that given sufficient time and generations, that it makes logical sense that micro changes can add up to macro changes. I get that! The difficulty for the theory of macroevolution (I am using the term as it is used in the literature for the mutation of one species into another species), is that there is no evidence! Where are the transitional forms? What we have are gaps in the process, missing links. And of late we have new theories that try to explain why we don't need such evidence.

But, be that as it may, that is not the point of my argument. You are arguing about the evidence and what it means. I am arguing about the fact that there is any evidence at all! My argument precedes the evidence. All of the evidence has to do with populations of species, and I am dealing with the origin of species, not adaptations within species. The argument of micro changes over lots of time does make logical sense. (Can you hear me now?) But there are two counts against it.

First, there is no evidence that one species can morph into another species in existence today. There is no historic evidence for it, nor is there any experimental evidence for it. Sure, populations of a species can adapt to various environmental conditions, but those variations do not produce a different species. Logically, they should! But they don't.

Second, there is the historical evidence of the Bible, which provides a story about the origins of life that better fit the evidence regarding speciation—that species were differentiated at the outset of time/creation by something beyond our understanding.

The argument is not about the evidence or the science. It's about philosophical method and cosmology, neither of which are available to scientific study. Science speculates about cosmology by studying astronomy and *theoretical* physics, but any serious scientist understands the *theoretical* nature of such study, and that the scientific method does not apply to cosmology. Nonetheless, there is huge edifice of scientific speculation that has been built around this topic in the hope of establishing "natural" causes regarding origins in order to undermine biblical fidelity.

What is a natural cause? Let's do a word analysis. *Natural* means "in accordance with nature." And nature means "a causal agent creating and controlling things in the universe." The whole Enlightenment idea of nature is the hope of determining causality without reference to a First Cause or God. This effort has spawned a kind of Godless language that is used in place of biblical language in order to discuss and determine what the Bible says that God alone has determined. It is an effort to escape from the authority of God, and God's demands for personal and social morality.

And this is your own desire, right? If there is no God, there is no absolute morality, no sin, no personal responsibility (except for what each individual personally values), no hell, etc. The purpose of the whole edifice of naturalism is to explain reality without reference to God, right? Such an effort is thought to be "objective" because it does not presuppose God. But the effort is not without presuppositions. It presupposes not-God, a world without God. But such an idea is as much a presupposition as is God. It is a theological belief because it posits a belief about God—that God doesn't exist. It is a theological position.

If God cannot be proven, which is true scientifically, then not-God cannot be scientifically proven either. Both are statements of theological belief. And your position of agnosticism is no better. Agnosticism is defined as "a religious orientation of doubt; a denial of ultimate knowledge of the existence of God," someone who is "uncertain of all claims to knowledge." Look it up yourself! It is a religious belief, not based on knowledge. And you want to claim that science supports it!

Get a grip! Be honest with yourself about it. You are espousing one religious view, and I am espousing another. By your own confession you are an unbeliever, and by mine I am a believer. You deny Christ, I affirm Christ. Isn't this the real bottom line?

Steven: "Steven, you used 'belief' because there is no other way to say what your relationship to evolution is."
The word "belief" applies to both of our positions in that we each accept the truth of our view. However, one of the definitions of the word "belief" is "religious faith: faith in God or a religion's god." In this sense, my understanding of evolution is not a belief. Since you reject evidentialism, you should have no problem seeing the difference between my understanding of evolution as a theory confirmed by mountains of evidence and your axiomatic assumption that a Trinitarian God created life largely in its current forms. The fact that the word "belief" can be applied to both of our stances in no way makes their foundations similar.

"If you have an interest in understanding the relationship between Christianity and science, you can read a book or two. Your desire for me to boil it down so you can shoot it down will only satisfy your lust for straw men to slay. I have given you sufficient information for serious inquiry."

You are unable to articulate how a faith-based worldview gave rise to an evidentialist worldview, so you suggest that I go read some books to understand it. I am going to call *bullsh*t* here and insist that if you can't articulate your own assertions, you shouldn't be making them. Your notion that I should go and put the pieces together for you is a cop out. Explain it or don't make the assertion.

Next, you say, "I understand the argument that given sufficient time and generations, that it makes logical sense that micro changes can add up to macro changes. I get that!" One becomes hopeful at this sentence that you may actually get it, but then you continue, "The difficulty for the theory of macroevolution (I am using the term as it is used in the literature for the mutation of one species into another species), is that there is no evidence!"

You once again demonstrate that you are spectacularly unread in the area of evolution. "Macroevolution" as used in the current scientific literature does not mean "speciation." Speciation can occur at the macro or micro evolutionary level. Rather "macroevolution" refers to evolution at or above the scale of gene pools. Please understand what you are criticizing.

You then make the tired, ludicrous creationist claim that "there is no evidence! Where are the transitional forms? What we have are gaps in the process, missing links. And of late we have new theories that try to explain why we don't need such evidence."

First of all, it is hypocritical and disingenuous for you to demand evidence. You are not an evidentialist. Even if mountains of evidence were thrown at you (which is actually the case right now) you would still dismiss them, would you not?

Your foundational assertion is that a Trinitarian God exists and all other ideas are subordinate to that. Why not be honest and just say, "yes the evidence points to evolution, but evidence doesn't matter. My faith-based world view is the correct one"?

But hypocrisy aside, you are dead wrong about this. Our museums are filled with transitional fossils. Here is an incomplete listing: Wikipedia.org/i/List_of_transitional_fossils. The approach creationists take when confronted with a transitional form is so transparently silly that I am surprised any of them can say it with a straight face. Rather than acknowledging the evidence, they ask "what about the forms in between the three you are showing?" To the creationist, when a fossil is found that is between two others, the gap is not filled, but two gaps now exist. Looking back at our bunny thought experiment, we can understand just how silly this is.

You then continue your hypocrisy by attacking evidence which should mean nothing to you in the first place.

"First, there is no evidence that one species can morph into another species in existence today. There is no historic evidence for it, nor is there any experimental evidence for it. Sure, populations of a species can adapt to various environmental conditions, but those variations do not produce a different species. Logically, they should! But they don't."

Yes they do. The evidence in genetics, geographic distribution of species and the geological fossil record are all cross-validating sources of evidence for this. You then propose a better "explanation" as follows:

"Second, there is the historical evidence of the Bible, which provides a story about the origins of life that better fit the evidence regarding speciation—that species were differentiated at the outset of time/creation by something beyond our understanding."

Again, the hypocrisy of turning to evidence. Let's leave that aside and follow your thought. The biblical story of the origins of life proposes that species were differentiated by "something beyond our understanding." How you can sincerely believe that what amounts to magic is a better explanation than anything is quite telling. Magic/mystery are not explanations of anything. This is why we must fight the introduction of creationism into science classrooms. It tells us that we should not bother trying to understand the origins of species and life. So very sad.

"The argument is not about the evidence or the science. It's about philosophical method and cosmology, neither of which are available to scientific study. Science speculates about cosmology by studying astronomy and theoretical physics, but any serious scientist understands the theoretical nature of such study, and that the scientific method does not apply to cosmology. Nonetheless, there is huge edifice of scientific speculation that has been built around this topic in the hope of establishing 'natural' causes regarding origins in order to undermine biblical fidelity."

Your claim that theoretical physics is not really science is specious. I have a feeling this is another area that you criticize without knowledge. Take a look at super colliders like the LHC and see how experimentation is used to refine theoretical models. Science.

"What is a natural cause? Let's do a word analysis. Natural means 'in accordance with nature.' And nature means 'a causal agent creating and controlling things in the universe.'"

No definition of nature specifies an agent. Please stick to American English definitions.

You say, "The purpose of the whole edifice of naturalism is to explain reality without reference to God, right?" Wrong. The purpose of naturalism is to use inductive reasoning and evidence to understand the world around us. If data were analyzed that pointed to a Trinitarian God, he would be put in the model.

You then say about naturalism: "It presupposes not-God, a world without God. But such an idea is as much a presupposition as is God. It is a theological belief because it posits a belief about God—that God doesn't exist. It is a theological position."

No it is not. Naturalism is based on an evidentialist epistemology. It does not say "there is no God." It says "there is data and evidence." I have heard this claim that every position is really theology. It is as ridiculous as saying that every activity is really scientific because you are either doing science or you are not.

You then say, "If God cannot be proven, which is true, then not-God cannot be proven either. Both are statements of theological belief." Right. Modern atheists do not firmly say "not-God." Nor do they say "not-unicorns" or "not-Russel's flying teapot" or "not-the Flying Spaghetti Monster." They do not assert the existence of any of those things because there is no reason to do so. What they do is base their world view on evidence and induction.

You then end strongly by saying, "Get a grip! Be honest with yourself about it. You are espousing one religious view, and I am espousing another. By your own confession you are an unbeliever, and by mine I am a believer. You deny Christ, I affirm Christ. Isn't this the real bottom line?"

I have not espoused a religious position to you. I am not sure why it is important to you to give my worldview that label. Is it pejorative?

Phillip: Steven, again you fail to see that we are talking about different things, and you most certainly fail to understand presuppositionalism.

Your claim and/or understanding that because I am a presuppositionalist I therefore have no consideration for evidence is specious. You have failed to understand that you and I disagree about what constitutes evidence and the interpretation of the evidence, not the existence of it.

"Evidence: Noun: The available body of facts or information indicating whether a belief or proposition is true or valid."

In the above definition, you and I disagree about what constitutes factuality, the meaning of information, the process of indication and the nature of truth. Our argument is not about the evidence itself, it's about evidence that I acknowledge (the veracity of the biblical witness) and you disallow. And its about the interpretation of the evidence, what it means.

You said that evolution is not a belief—correct. It is a theory about life and the origin of life, as you acknowledge. Theories are not facts, but are attempts to organize facts. I'm not disagreeing about the existence of the evidence, but the interpretation of it. I'm also suggesting that there is much more evidence involved than the material evidence. There is also the biblical and historical evidence that you disallow. I call it evidence and factor it in, but you don't and factor it out.

So, you are calling the suggestion to read about how Christianity gave rise to science bullsh*t. Then you accuse me of being narrow-minded and blind to the facts. What can I say? Wow. It seems that you have no interest in Christianity, so reading or learning about it are out. Interesting.

"Speciate: Evolve so as to lead to a new species or develop in a way most suited to the environment." I use the WordWeb dictionary most of the time.

I used the term and defined it "as it is used in the literature for the mutation of one species into another species." Yet, you accuse me of assertion, but the assertions are not mine. I'm simply using them. For instance (from Wikipedia),

"Within the Modern Synthesis school of thought, macroevolution is thought of as the compounded effects of microevolution. [7] Thus, the distinction between micro- and macroevolution is not a fundamental one—the only difference between them is of time and scale." The only difference between them is the magic sauce of time!

"A more practical definition of the term describes it as changes occurring on geological time scales, in contrast to microevolution, which occurs on the timescale of human lifetimes. [6] This definition reflects the spectrum between micro- and macro-evolution, whilst leaving a clear difference between the terms: because the geological record rarely has a resolution better than 10,000 years, and humans rarely live longer than 100 years, 'meso-evolution' is never observed."

Here we see that the time sauce has poor resolution, and nothing other than microevolution is ever observed. This is not my assertion, it's right out of Wikipedia / Macroevolution.

I'm not demanding evidence for my sake. I'm demanding it because you are the evidentialist, yet you fail to acknowledge that the evidence is speculative. And for an evidentialist to rely on speculative evidence is contrary to the principles of evidentialism.

I do not dismiss the evidence "thrown at me." I interpret it differently because I acknowledge that there is other evidence that impacts the case that you disallow. When you say "Looking back at our bunny thought experiment, we can understand just how silly this is," do you mean that the "impossible" bunny thought experiment is "evidence" of something? Isn't a bunny thought experiment a kind of speculation?

I do in fact continue to attack your ideas about what constitutes evidence, but this is not an indication of any hypocrisy on my part. It is quite consistent with my stated beliefs and methods. But you are trying to turn what should be a legitimate discussion about the definition of evidence into an *ad hominem* personal attack on my character—accusing me of hypocrisy. You should know better than that.

Your paragraph on magic/mystery is at the heart of our difference. I suspect that you think that I equate magic and mystery as you seem to. But I don't. There is quite a difference between them, and the difference is similar to the difference between evidentialism and presuppositionalism. Your misunderstanding and disallowance of the biblical literature to provide any sort of evidence or facts causes you to disregard the role of axiomatic evidence.

This means that you are blind to it, you don't see it, and not seeing it, you don't believe that it exists, and not believing that it exists, you disregard what I say about it. And call me names for mentioning it. But because I understand the difference between magic and mystery, I am even more opposed to magic than you are. But because you conflate the terms, you cannot understand this.

My definition of nature comes from WordWeb. But why the rant against the idea that nature suggests a causal agent? The American Heritage Dictionary defines nature as "The forces and processes that produce and control all the phenomena of the material world." Aren't these forces and processes causing phenomena? Can't a force or a process act as an agent? Methinks that thou protestest against the personal nature of thy God overly much.

The difference between "not asserting the existence of" and "asserting the non-existence of" is logically chimerical. Modern atheists seem to deny the definition of atheism. "A," which means "not" and "theist," from "theism," which is "The doctrine or belief in the existence of a God or gods." Atheism is a position with regard to the existence of God, which then makes it a kind of theism. Mathematically, it corresponds to a belief in the number of gods that exist, i.e. zero, one, two, three or more, where zero is a number, which includes atheism in the general category of theism. But this fact is denied because atheists do not see any reason to grant any acknowledgment whatsoever to God or the idea of god. And not seeing, they deny it.

Indeed, your worldview is pejorative to God (Psalm 14:1, 53:1, 92:6; Proverbs 10:8, 12:15, 13:16, 17:24, 18:2, 26:12, 28:26; 1 Corinthians 1:20).

Steven:
"*Axiomatic evidence!*" [Facepalm.]
I think we might be done here. I understand your view quite well. It is fundamentally inconsistent with science. I think you understand my world view. It is fundamentally inconsistent with faith-based presuppositionalism. We have reached the heart of the matter and I believe we are at an impasse. You will go on attacking science and I will go on defending it. I hope for the human race that my side wins, but who knows?

Phillip: Steven, I agree that we are at an impasse, but I disagree with your assessment about what the impasse is. Your thinking that my view is inconsistent with science stands as evidence that you do not understand my view or the Bible or philosophy. I am not attacking science, nor am I attacking you. I am attacking godlessness. And I have no doubt that God knows which side will win this argument (Psalm 2:4). Truth always wins in the long run.

It has been a good joust, and I am all the more confident because it. Thanks for providing a committed layman's statement of your view. And be assured that you will continue to be on my prayer list.

Steven: Phillip, you said "Your thinking that my view is inconsistent with science stands as evidence that you do not understand my view or the Bible or philosophy."

You have stated that the foundation of modern biology is incorrect and that we should rightly understand the origin of species as being caused by a mysterious force we cannot understand. Much as you may not like it, this view is inconsistent with science. As for me not understanding your position, read back in the thread. I restated the fundamentals of it in my own words and you said I was correct.

Phillip: Steven, I said that you had done a fine job of summing up my position, and have pointed out the errors inherent in reductionism—even pointed you to helpful books on the subject. Previously, I also pointed out that your words were like those of Baalam—correct, but empty of reality. Your "understanding" is like a kid in school who crams for the test, remembering key phrases and such. He takes the test and passes, but has no interest in the subject and doesn't really understand the words he has memorized, and doesn't care about it. You simply regurgitated what I said, so you could accuse me of various things.

Again, to the point of our disagreement, I did say that the origin of the species comes from God who is ultimately a mystery. But I did not say that we can understand nothing of God. Apparently, you can't, but others can. We can understand much of what God has said. The mystery is that we are not gods, nor infinite ourselves, so we cannot fully understand all of God. The difference is the critical element that differentiates the saved from the lost.

"I have given her time to repent of her immorality, but she is unwilling" (Revelation 2:21).

Postscript

Whew! What was that about?

That is likely a common response to such an argument. I was pleased that Stephen was willing to remain engaged for such a long time. On the one hand, serious arguments suffer when they happen in the moment because careful responses take time to formulate. They tend to be reduced to issues that are not related to the actual argument. But on the other hand, written arguments like this one tend to be too abstract and get lost in the weeds of technicalities.

This discussion was about the trustworthiness of the Bible and the character of God. The issues engaged (homosexuality, evolution, science, etc.), while important, provide each side with conclusions that are argued from, rather than determinations to which the arguments conclude. As long as the sides are arguing against one another, no commonly agreed upon winner can emerge. The only way for such an argument as this to come to a real conclusion is for the disputants to argue with God rather than with one another. Only God can win an argument like this because the argument is really about God Himself. Both sides are really arguing with God, arguing about who God really is, what He really teaches in the Bible, and what He wants from people. Christians argue that God is real and wants genuine love and respect, atheists argue that God is nothing and wants nothing. And in an argument like this both sides have much to learn. Each can learn from the other, and both can—and must—learn from God Himself.

The underlying argument concerns epistemology, the philosophical study of what distinguishes justified belief from mere opinion. How do we know that what we think we know is actually true? At the center of epistemology lies belief and faith, which issue out of our most fundamental presuppositions. It is quite difficult to examine one's own assumptions because assumptions are taken for granted. For the most part they are unexamined, and the process of examining them removes their assumptiveness. To question an assumption is to stop assuming it, not necessarily to stop believing it, but no longer assuming its truth. To seriously question one's own assumptions is to question one's own identity and character. The more seriously it is done, the deeper it goes, the more threatening it becomes to our false ideas about who we think we are, about our strengths and weaknesses, even our likes and dislikes—our preferences.

We tend to think that we know who we are because we think we have always been who we think we are. But in reality we cannot know who we actually are as individuals *in and of ourselves* because we are social beings. Individual identity is socially constructed. We learn about ourselves by interacting with others. For the most part our idea of our own personal identity comes from the culture in which we live. Human beings are the most adaptable species to inhabit this planet. Our adaptability is one of our greatest strengths, but it is also one of our greatest weaknesses. It may be that we mistake our human adaptability for evolution, but that's another discussion.

It is not just that we are a "monkey see, monkey do" people, but that the ability to imitate is at the very core of life itself. Think DNA, the complex concatenation of molecules that provide the instructions that literally define every living thing. The longevity and precision of DNA replication is beyond both calculation and imagination.

Life itself appears to be fractal.[1] Other magnitudes of scale are not directly available to us experientially, nonetheless we can posit them mathematically, though the math itself is beyond the abilities of most people to understand. But again, just because something is beyond our comprehension does not mean that it is not real. Life replicates itself. Humanity replicates itself. Individuals replicate themselves. And fractal geometry suggests the math that may be involved in such replication, which in turn opens up other avenues of philosophical inquiry that are quite interesting, meaningful, and spiritually allusive.

But what is the right model upon which to replicate human character? The Bible teaches that people imitate God, that we become like what we worship, what we honor, what we value. Adam and Eve honored themselves above God, their own ability to know right from wrong—and humanity has sinfully followed their lead. That's what people do, and that's our primary problem because we actually don't know what we are doing with regard to morality most of the time. People are like individual events in the larger story of life, and the individual events or life-stories interact to become the larger story of the culture. And what is needed is for the larger story of the culture to have purpose, meaning, and substance. Without such a viable story, individuals languish.

Evolution & Story

Evolution is not a fact, nor an event. It is a story. The same is true about the biblical story of creation in Genesis. Both creationists and evolutionists provide an explanation of human origins. Both explanations are stories. The Bible teaches that God created humanity five to seven thousand years ago. Science teaches that

---

1   Fractal: a curve or geometric figure, each part of which has the same statistical character as the whole. Fractals are useful in modeling structures (such as eroded coastlines or snowflakes) in which similar patterns recur at progressively smaller scales, and in describing partly random or chaotic phenomena such as crystal growth, fluid turbulence, and galaxy formation.

the universe began when a singularity exploded about fourteen billion years ago. I don't see any reason to reject either story, though I have some questions about time. Nor or do I believe that the biblical story is talking about the same thing as the scientific, evolutionary story.

While both are stories about the creation of the universe, or about life in the universe, they define and use the word *universe* differently. Science defines *universe* as the stars and galaxies at the very large end of the scale, and atoms, protons, etc. at the very small end—the material stuff the universe is made of. Evolutionary scientists tend to refer to the *thing signified* by the story of evolution. But the Bible is talking about the descriptive, linguistic, conceptual, and cultural apparatus through which we perceive the universe—the *sign* that points to it. The Bible defines *universe* linguistically as the consciousness or awareness with which perception is possible, not the *stuff* of the universe, but the *story* of the universe, the *uni*tary character of the *verse*, the story of human existence. Science examines the data, the physics, while Scripture examines the metadata, the metaphysics. Science is looking at the object(s) of our perception, while Scripture is looking at the means of our perception.

This idea is hardly new or groundbreaking, but it has been lost in the contemporary world because of our fascination with technology and the new data technology has provided. Metaphysics got a bad rap in the early modern era because the newly discovered sciences and their technologies were too blunt to provide cogent metadata information about the material world. But the new technological instruments today have opened up both the heavens (the realm of the very large) and the earth (the realm of the very small) to better scientific examination. Contemporary instrumentation has produced meaningful metadata, and is revolutionizing the study of metaphysics.[2]

---

2 http://www.colorado.edu/philosophy/vstenger/Quantum/qmeta.html. Also, Delio, Ilia. *The Unbearable Wholeness of Being: God, Evolution, and the Power of Love*, Orbis Books, 2013. Delio has pulled together a lot of material from a lot

There is no shortage of supply of contemporary metaphysical books that are trying to tap into religious roots of all sorts, all traditions. Among the best of these Christian authors is Ilia Delio, a Roman Catholic Franciscan, who has woven together a plethora of metaphysical sources and ideas to prop up the work of Pierre Teilhard de Chardin, one of the early new metaphysicians who wrote during the first half of the twentieth century. Tielhard has much to offer to both theology and science. However, Tielhard was not sufficiently careful in his use of the theological categories of Christ's dual nature, His divinity and His humanity. Tielhard fails to sufficiently distinguish them, which blurs and confuses the uniqueness of Jesus Christ and the pervasiveness and tenacity of human sin.

Much of the contemporary enthusiasm for evolution is coming from an effort to merge the new scientific and technological metadata with various religious ideas. However, the effort continues to import religious ideas into scientific evolutionary categories as a way to bolster the scientific theories. The metadata is being used to justify the story of scientific evolution. Even those who embrace some version of Christian evolution or intelligent design are trying to use God or the Bible to justify the story of scientific, material evolution.

The whole endeavor is wrongheaded from a Christian perspective because it uses the story of scientific evolution as the primary source, rather than the biblical story of creation in the light of Christ as the primary source. To be faithful to Scripture we must use the Bible as the foundational source upon which to engage the new scientific and technological metadata. And one of the most fruitful ways to do this will be to realize that the scientific story of our origins and the biblical story of our origins are not about the same things. Again, scientific evolution is about the data, where the biblical story of creation is about the metadata.

---

of sources, and has a bibliography.

This issue is very much like the idea of mistaking symbol for reality that is discussed in my book on Galatians.[3] This confusion is also the source of idolatry, where at a lower level, statues are mistaken for God, and at a higher level ideas are mistaken for the realities they symbolize. It involves a confusion of the sign with the thing signified, of the map for the terrain, of the computer modeling for some actual reality.

In the case of evolution, people mistake the description of the physics for the reality of the thing described. They think that the metadata of physics is of the same stuff as physics, or on the same plane, or in the same orbit, etc. Consequently, they think that the object of study is material reality rather than the realm of psycho-social-spiritual cognition and the relationship between symbol and reality.[4] Our study of the world is as much about ourselves as it is about the world—perhaps even more so because of our tendency and the historical tenacity of this categorical error to persist.

The Bible is about "seeing" God, who cannot be "seen," yet is "seen" in the face of Jesus Christ. The Bible is the story of God's activity in our world and in our lives, as He increasingly comes to be "seen" through His people. The Advent of Jesus Christ created a worldwide revolution of culture that is still unfolding. Jesus came to inaugurate the actual manifestation of God in the world, and He will return at its completion. Jesus inaugurated a new way of thinking about God, the world, and ourselves. That new way of thinking can be considered to be religious, and His intention is to replace the old way of thinking with the new way, the Old Testament with the New Testament. As this new way of thinking and "seeing" ourselves, the world, and God becomes predominant the revolution that Jesus began will become

---

3   Ross, Phillip A. *Galatians—Backstoty/Christory*, Pilgrim Platform, Marietta, Ohio, 2015.
4   Pannenberg, Wolfhart. *Faith & Reality*, Westminster Press, Philadelphia, 1977.

established, not simply codified into law, but deep-rooted in the hearts and minds of people everywhere.

This revolution has already changed the world more than it has ever changed before Christ, and quite honestly, the change has barely begun. However, it is not really the world that is changing, it is us—humanity. We are adapting to Christ. The worldwide revolution that Jesus inaugurated is not really about changing the world, it's about changing us, changing our understanding of who God is, who we are, and what the world is. We are not who we have traditionally thought ourselves to be, nor is God who we have traditionally understood Him to be, nor is the world what our ancestors understood it to be. The old way, the old ways of thinking about ourselves, our world, and God are not wrong—but they are inadequate to the new realities that are now being "seen." We are, however, who the Bible shows us to be. God is who the Bible says He is. And the world is what the Bible says that it is.

From this perspective then, evolution is not about the environment. It's not about how the world or other species are changing. It's about us, about humanity, and about our psycho-social-spiritual cognition. From a Christian perspective, it's about our sanctification, our growth in Christ—and *sanctification* would be a much better word to use. However, it is not that we are evolving into some sort of super being or super species. Rather, we are growing into what God created us to be in Christ. Jesus inaugurated a new humanity, a new way of being human that is replacing the old humanity in Adam. But to call it "evolution" puts it on the wrong foundation. It's not primarily about science. It's not grounded in science. It's about God, and about us, about history. It's about people. It is much better to call it what the Bible knows it to be: sanctification, or maturity in Christ.

The idea of changing the world, of making a difference, suggests that what needs to change is not us, but the world. The evolutionary idea is to make the world more fit for people like us by changing *it*, when the real need is to make ourselves more fit to live in the world that God gave us, the only world that we can live in. The world is not out of sorts, we are! The problem is not that there is too much pollution in the world, or that there are too many people for the world to support. Rather, the problem is what we believe about the world and the way we live. The problem is that there is too much sin. The answer to the pollution problem is not to install more and better industrial smoke stack scrubbers, but to reduce and eliminate the need for industrial smoke stack scrubbers. What needs to change is not simply how we produce stuff, but the entire structure of our lives and society.

Western culture has given us some fantastic science and technology, but because early scientists were unable to agree about the metadata (metaphysics) of science, we either abandoned the study of metaphysics altogether, or following Kant, we created a special intellectual area for it. Consequently, the area of study that is most able to unify human understanding was cordoned off from reality in order to protect the "purity" of science from the metaphysics of another era. A wall of separation was erected between science and metaphysics, between science and the metadata of science, between science and religion, between science and the Bible.

Modern science then developed a technology that created a worldwide culture based on this fundamental bifurcation of reality that results from the confusion of symbol and reality. The problems that have been created by Western, scientific culture are many. And because our philosophical approach to science, technology, and education has been divisive, by which I mean specialized, our approach to the myriad of problems has also been specialized—and divisive. However, it is the divisiveness of our specialized approach to the problems we have created that keeps us from addressing the essential problem from a holistic perspective. The thing that we need most is a metaphysics that is commensurate with the current state of physics.

Cultures issue from common stories, and the story of Western civilization is competitive, divisive, fragmented, and partial.

So it has created people who are competitive, divisive, fragmented, and partial. The need of the hour is to rediscover human cooperation and wholeness, the harmonious place of humanity in the universe, and the wholeness of being that is best described as union with Christ. And because Jesus Christ started the worldwide revolution in human culture that has brought us to this point, and because the Bible was written precisely for such a time as this, Jesus Christ is uniquely able to provide what we need. Could it be that God knew from the very beginning of recorded history that humanity would come to this very point in our history, to this present crisis, and has provided a remedy? Could it be that we are not the first culture on earth or in the universe to have run into this problem of cultural adaptation to rapidly advancing technological progress?

The need of the hour is not to abandon the Bible because a poor understanding of it puts it into conflict with a poor understanding of science. What is needed is not to try to conform or justify the Bible with science, but to see the metadata of contemporary science in the light of the Bible through the eyes of Christ. Every generation must understand the Bible for themselves without abandoning or contradicting the orthodox history of biblical wisdom. The Bible doesn't change, but we do—and if we don't, then God's plan has failed! However, we do not become anything other than what we were created to be in Christ. In Christ we are guided by the infinite creativity of God Himself, and we discover new ways to faithfully understand His Word by standing on the shoulders of those faithful Christians who have gone before us.

The kingdom of God will not suddenly drop out of the sky like some kind of UFO invasion. The kingdom of God has been growing on the earth for a very long time, and like all living things it grows in cycles and seasons, waxing and waning, but over time increasing in size, quality, and meaning. The seed is not like the blade, nor is the blade like the ear, yet the seed, blade, and ear are all one plant. Similarly, the Father is not the Son, nor is the Son the Holy Spirit, yet Father, Son, and Holy Spirit are one.[5] The past is not like the present, nor is the present like the future will be. Yet, there is a consistent story that unites past, present, and future; Father, Son, and Holy Spirit; seed, blade, and ear.

> "You won't be able to say, 'Here it is!' or 'It's over there!' For the Kingdom of God is already among you" (Luke 17:21, *New Living Translation*).

---

5 The Trinity is at the heart of both Christianity and science. More about this can be found in many of my books.

Appendix

Definition of Marriage, 2010

The definition of terms always determines the shape and conclusion of an argument, case, statement, or policy, assuming that it unfolds logically. Thus, the definition of marriage is the central concern in the debate about so-called gay marriage.

However, as soon as the issue is referred to as "gay marriage" its definition is influenced by the preposition "gay." To consider "gay marriage" at all is to assume that there are various types of marriage, "gay marriage" being one of them. But such thinking contradicts common dictionaries, common traditions, common practices, common law, and common sense.

To define a thing requires going to its root or genesis. Where did the thing come from? What is its purpose? What has been its history? And lastly what is the common understanding of the thing in contemporary society?

Marriage finds its origin in the Bible. Of course, people are free to disregard the Bible, but in doing so they disregard the historic traditions of Christianity, Judaism, Islam and the foundation of America's legal system (at least its first 200 years). In the United States the combined adherence of these religious traditions represents a very healthy majority opinion, should majority opinions count for anything in America. So, if this majority is to discuss the issue of "gay marriage," they should call it by its biblical and historic name — sodomy.

The American Heritage Dictionary defines "sodomy" as "1. Anal copulation of one male with another. 2. Anal or oral copulation with a member of the opposite sex. 3. Copulation with an animal." The same dictionary defines "sodomite" as one who engages in sodomy. The long history of sodomy is dark and full of deceit.

To engage in sodomy is to use a thing (sex) in a manner that is contrary to its fundamental purpose (procreation). Sodomy, then, has no social purpose or function. It is simply an activity of personal sexual self-gratification. And consenting adults are free to engage it in the privacy of their own homes, unless they claim biblical fidelity or children are involved.

The purpose of biblical—and, therefore, traditional—marriage, on the other hand, is procreation within families. Thus, the normal product of marriage—family—has been called the cradle of civilization. Children are best raised in healthy families composed of a mother and a father (to provide a balance of normal sexual role models) who have covenanted together in the promise to remain together for life for the sake of the betterment of their children and their society.

How does biblical marriage contribute to the betterment of children and society? By modeling normal (procreative) sex roles, representative government and the importance of the integrity of social contracts.

Biblical marriage, however, is not merely a social contract between two people. It involves a contract with God, who forbids sodomy. Similarly, civil marriage (a relatively recent invention) involves a contract with the state. The state is a party involved in civil marriage because the state claims an interest in the welfare of families.

But does the state have an interest in personal sexual self-gratification? Recent court decisions have already redefined the family in an attempt to legitimize sodomy. But what interest does the state have in sodomy, since by definition it cannot produce offspring? Does the state consider sodomy a legitimate form of birth control? Does the pursuit of happiness guarantee the right to engage in sodomy? And if so, why should children be exempt from such a right? Does the state have the right to undermine and destroy traditionally biblically-based families?

Families are biologically related social units. Of course, adoption is a legitimate element of family constitution, but it is the exception rather than the norm. Definitions ought to be based upon norms, while allowing for exceptions, and not based upon exceptions to the norm.

To accept state sanctioned sodomy will drive a serious wedge between biblical government (instituted in part through families) and civil government that will have very serious consequences for society because at the point that the state legitimizes (encourages) sodomy the majority of citizens (those claiming adherence to Christianity, Judaism, Islam, and the historic foundation of the American legal system) will find themselves in an irreconcilable disagreement with their own government. They will be threatened by the fact that their government will actively and intentionally undermine and destroy the very foundations of biblical society — the biblically defined and regulated family.

It almost appears that someone's behind-the-scenes strategy is to cause the American people such distress with their government that they will abide the dismantling (or redefining) of the Constitution. Sodomites have always been political pawns in the game of dismantling nations.

The problem is not the Constitution, but the ongoing failure to abide by it. Similarly, the problem is not the legal definition of marriage, but the failure to abide by it. More broadly, the problem is not the traditional biblical perspective, but the failure to abide by it.

Welcome to the age of American anarchy.

The Church & The Future—An Essay

We who are in the church, especially pastors and denominational executives, have a vested interest in maintaining the church as it currently exists. Of course we'd like our church and/or denomination to grow, but what we mean is that we would like more of what it already is, more of the same kind of people, more resources, etc. What we really want is a better status quo, churches like the ones we have, but bigger. But is that what God wants or what God is doing at this time in history? It doesn't seem to be. The church plural is in crisis. I don't have a magic solution for this problem, but it is worth discussing, worth facing up to some harsh realities, and taking stock. Which is better: harsh realities or false hope?

The change that is needed must involve the top, the leaders. If the church were a corporation, that change would come in the form of new leadership. Of course churches and denominations do that all the time by getting new leaders. It usually involves firing and hiring, and churches have been doing that for eons, with little to show for it. We mostly get more of the same—better packaged, more efficient, different way to maintain the same status quo. The new leaders believe the same things. Most of what has been happening in America in the past fifty years is church consolidation. Small churches are folding, and large churches are getting larger, while overall market share continues to be lost. It's time to ask if that is really what God wants.

But how can we who have a vested interest (pastors, denominational leaders, church leaders who depend for our livelihood on the church as we know it) even consider any alternatives (or truths) that would undermine our vested interests or positions of leadership? We need something radically new—or perhaps the renewal of something very old, something largely forgotten and of little consideration in our fast paced lives.

One of the themes of much of my writing deals with various misunderstandings of Scripture that cause us to beat dead horses in the hope of taking the gospel to the world. Most evangelism efforts are still couched in the language of the Second Great Awakening, which is of little interest to the younger generations, and puts the older generations asleep because they have heard it all before.

The language of Christian liberalism is in direct opposition to this language, and therefore is equally handicapped and equally dependent upon it—but is even more lethargic. The Fundamentalists and Evangelicals are locked in a theological battle with the Mainline Liberals, which is just where Satan would like us to be. All of our energy and attention are consumed in struggling with one another. The struggle is not as enthusiastic as it used to be, so our energies wax and wane between trying to work up enough enthusiasm to care, or letting our differences languish in the bureaucratic language of ecumenism.

For instance, we (pastors, denominational leaders, and church leaders) have a vested interest in church property (buildings and bank accounts – cash flow). But to what extent do we limit (and harm) the gospel by forcing the Spirit to work through the channels of finance? To what extent do our vested interests actually impede genuine gospel expansion? It's like we are trying to wrestle the Holy Spirit into our churches, rather than allowing the Holy Spirit to lead us wheresoever He will.

The world is hungry for the gospel, but a very large number of people can't or won't connect with it through "traditional" channels (churches, denominations, missions). If the gospel is going to reach the majority of people, and if by "reach" we mean that people must be connected to "traditional" churches and denominations, we won't be able to build enough churches fast enough to meet the real need. And all of our energies will be inward directed toward more materialistic stuff. Rather than working to get people into church, we need to work to get Christ's church into people. As long as we are focused on maintaining, expanding, and improving the churches, we are focused on doing more of the same thing—which isn't working very well, at least not as well as it needs to work to meet the need.

We need to turn our attention to the larger culture, get out attention out of the confines of the ghettoized churches. The idea that the church is supposed to provide an alternative culture produces an insular Christianity. It quarantines the church from society, which is exactly what the culture of sin wants the church to be! The church is not to be an alternative way of life in a world filled with sin (which is a common view among pastors, churches, and denominations). Rather, the church is to be the engine of culture—the primary driving force of culture. The church (God's people) and biblical wisdom should be at the cutting edges of education, science, technology, and finance. The church is a mindset, a worldview, a way of life, not an institution, building, or social organization. It is life itself, not just something to do on Sunday mornings.

Unfortunately, church theology is stuck in the 19th, or the 16th, or the 7th, or the 4th, or the 1st century, depending on your preferred tradition. We look to the past for guidance into the future, as if the ideal is to make the future like the past. The church (pastors, denominational leaders, and church leaders) are not on the cutting edge of anything in sufficient numbers, but are overwhelmingly in the ghettos. Which is why the vast majority of pastors are discouraged and languishing! We like to draw our hope from the ministry "successes" who are doing very well, who have large churches and large followings. But doing that only compounds our problems for several reasons. First, large churches tend to be good at worldly success, which the New Testament spends much ink opposing. So, modeling our efforts on "what's working" will bring success to a few more large churches, but not to the gospel of Jesus Christ, the suffering servant who sacrificed His life for us. Suffering and sacrifice are hard to sell. We don't understand that worldly success is not our friend.

The answer is not building more churches, or growing existing churches and denominations, or starting new churches and denominations on the model of "what works." We don't need larger, more effective, and better funded Christian ghettos. The idea that the church is a hospital in the midst of a sick and sinful world is fine. But the mission of a hospital is not to get more people into its beds. Rather, the greater mission is to get them out of bed and keep them out of the hospital. The church needs to work to keep people out of the hospital, not work to get more people into it. The church needs to become proactive in its healing mission, and not just heal the brokenhearted. The church must address the causes of sin and illness – most of which are self-inflicted, just as most physical health problems result from bad choices and wrong lifestyles. As Pogo once said: I have met the enemy, and they are us!

If it is we—the church—who are the problem, then it is we who must change. And for leaders to lead us in the right changes, we must have rightly changed leaders. But what changes? And how can we make the needed changes? The first step to solving any problem is to recognize the problem as a problem. Scripture drives the churches, or it should! So, the solution is to reconnect with the drive train in the right way, to reunderstand the Bible—Old Testament and New, to see the old truths with new eyes. This is what I write about, so if you want to know more, that's where you can find it.

www.ingramcontent.com/pod-product-compliance
Lightning Source LLC
Chambersburg PA
CBHW071508040426
42444CB00008B/1554